The TRUMP We Love To LOVE!

Alexa Keating

Copyright © 2020 Alexa Keating

All rights reserved.

ISBN: 9798690695651

DEDICATION

'The Trump We Love to LOVE' is dedicated to every American who set aside their preconceived ideas about who could and should lead our nation and looked long and hard to determine the best path forward. Those who were willing to take a chance on a man with no political background may very well have saved the America we all love. Thank you.

CONTENTS

	The Mystique Of Donald Trump	i
1	We LOVE You!	1
2	The Cracks Begin	14
3	A Charismatic Leader Emerges	18
4	A Rising Tide	23
5	The Gates Unguarded	27
6	A New Day Dawns	33
7	Extreme Justice	39
8	The Price of 'Parxit'	46
9	**The Witches Brew**	**52**
10	The Parade Of Shams	56
11	A New Horizon As the Engine Roars	64
12	Mighty Might	69
13	Promises Made Promises Kept	74
14	Chinas Calling Card	79
15	From Chaos to Clarity	88
16	Loud and Proud	93
	About the Author	99

THE MYSTIQUE OF DONALD TRUMP

Donald Trump is an enigma that all of us can learn from. He is 'cool' enough to attract the attention of our youth while retaining the old fashioned ideals that made our country the shining beacon of light on the hill. We all had our thoughts about the man he must be, mostly based on articles we have read and stories we have heard. He is a successful businessman, a billionaire whose extravagant lifestyle may have been more imagined than real.

We learned over time that he worked far more than he played and that he was a strict father who demanded obedience and a good work ethic from his children. He taught by example. For his own personal reasons he avoided alcohol and drugs in a life where either would have been easy to embrace. Donald Trump has a history that includes great public losses but far more wins in his column. The losses were likely his best teacher.

Americans have been treated to four years of information we never hoped to learn about our Federal Government and the corruption that had overtaken it. As we learned these facts we were also treated to an example of how to stand tall and keep your shoulder to the wheel to move things forward.

Donald Trump reminded us of why grit and perseverance are essential to winning. Like the giant Sequoia he refused to be felled by lies and bitter attacks. He has traversed a path from open scorn to crowds chanting 'We LOVE You!' It was this that inspired me to write a story about a man who has earned the right to be addressed as, 'To Sir with Love!'

1 WE LOVE YOU!

'We love YOU! We love YOU!' Shocking, these chants are heard in unison by tens of thousands of people excitedly supporting the most unlikely of speakers; Donald John Trump, the 45th President of the United States of America.

The shock effect has passed now as it has become commonplace to witness the excited words repeated loudly from a crowd of literally tens of thousands of people. Maybe equally difficult to understand is that these enormous crowds have gathered without coercion to listen raptly to a man they can easily see and hear on television almost daily. And yet, they do come, many times days in advance, to secure a favorable vantage point waiting for the moment when he appears. Thunderous applause greets Donald Trump; he is a true phenomenon.

Whether Donald Trump is 'in the house' for a rally or departing from Air Force 1 and approaching an outdoor crowd, he is greeted like a rock star. To many, many people he is far beyond the rock star status. Is this strange?

In the past many politicians' campaigns offered free busing to create an illusion that a few hundred people supported them. They were gathered and placed on display by the news media for the world to see. In the 'monkey see, monkey do' tradition, they hoped you would believe that these strangers who followed them indicated that you too must make the same choice.

Politics has not treated President Donald John Trump kindly; he was the surgical procedure for a disease that most Americans had become all too aware of. 'We the people' had come to the realization that those they had chosen in good faith had, for many years, utterly betrayed them. Our elected officials had sold their integrity to the highest bidder, and worse.

Political parties were fractured as one party pursued identity politics with a strong bend towards Socialism; while the other simply refused to attend the reckoning. The people had become increasingly disenchanted with both parties. The parties went to extreme efforts to ensure they would never be forced to answer for their compliant surrender to ideas that could never benefit the people who had elected them.

Donald J. Trump was exposing their willingness to trade the single greatest human experiment in the history of mankind, The United States of America, for the concept of a globalist planet where none but a few could prosper or pursue a personal dream. It was earth shattering.

Those in power and those who were certain they would assume power believed that 'We the people' must never, ever know the only possible destination of the road we were traveling was one of utter destruction of our birthright as an American citizen.

Understandably, this was a *very* closed society among those identifying as the 'elite.' This group of liberals and ultra-far left people have gathered under the umbrella of the Democrats. They fully intended to take over that party. In their arrogance they failed to notice that the very word 'elite' would be looked upon with utter disdain by their fellow Americans.

These elitists were a tight knit club with a mantra of 'don't ask, don't tell.'

This was utterly necessary for two distinct reasons; 'We the people' would never knowingly capitulate to losing the country we loved to the very thing its immigrants had fled. Secondly, the money and power that supported their campaigns demanded their compliance. They had a plan… one that did not include the people

This powerful group of elitist had forgotten that their imagined position of greatness they so cherished had been gained upon the backs of those they believed had so little value.

This was not a new concept or movement; it was instead an infected sore that had been festering for more than half a century. Slowly, slowly, like water dripping onto a rock, their intolerance of free speech joined an evil pursuit of identity politics. Smears and jeers turned into violence with rampant finger pointing if the American people dared to protest. Suddenly a litany of 'ists,' 'isms' and 'phobias' rained down upon the heads of those who dared to call out this obvious demise of values and beliefs that had made America strong. 'How dare these underlings notice or accuse those who had diligently worked for half a century to approach their goal line!' What finally emerged was a clear intention to bring American exceptionalism to its knees.

Complacency had set in with the citizens of America. We soon found ourselves looking the other way at ideas we knew were destroying the moral foundation of our country. Silently we thought these ideas were really far out, but most Americans simply allowed things to pass. We expected that our leaders would never allow our freedom to be compromised or taken from us. We had mistakenly assumed we had the same goals.

Soon, very little attention was focused on the people and how they felt. It was their duty to shut up and suffer. The perpetrators of the new globalist pursuit genuinely believed that America had risen to unfair heights and therefore must pay; everything they stood for must be sacrificed. The people must be broken so they would be willing to surrender.

If there were voices of political leaders who had dared to comment on these events, they were drowned out by the hate filled, bitter people. It would take a thundering voice with ruthless abandon to beat back this effort to surrender America to the ruins they believed she deserved.

Then one day in June of 2015 as the people sat in their living rooms, many feeling defeated, we were treated to the scene of an escalator descending in New York City. Never has such a scene been so deeply imprinted into the memory of millions of people. This day would never be forgotten.. There on that descending escalator was a soft spoken, brash and very tough New York billionaire builder, businessman and entertainer accompanied by his beautiful wife; both smiling broadly. The model and the man known as Donald John Trump had descended upon the political scene of the USA.

With no written speech in hand and no 'handlers' beside him this man known as 'The Donald' promptly walked to the microphone and announced that he was running for the office of President of the United States of America. He quickly set about accurately identifying approaching dangers; those same ones the American people had long been suspecting could destroy them.

Americans had had been 'sold out' he told them. Gone was the country they had long believed was a shining example to the world. It had been replaced by globalism. Their freedom to profoundly believe in their own control of their future had been bartered for bits and pieces of the American Dream. Their heritage as a citizen had been sold for things they had never agreed to. The people had been right! It was exactly as they had suspected.

After years of utter boredom in American politics, the people were understandably enticed by this event. For many years they had invited this man into their homes weekly; they felt they knew him in some way, even trusted his instincts. But Donald Trump in politics; this was new to them. And so, they listened.

For those who had any real interest in politics, this announcement was not utterly shocking. Donald Trump had always been interested in events occurring in America, and somewhat involved. Ronald Reagan famously shook his hand many years ago and remarked that he felt he was shaking the hand of a future President.

The Donald had long been warning Americans of the impending dangers approaching them, persistently voicing his concern. Oprah Winfrey once asked him if he would run for President one day. His response was, 'Only if my country needs me.' That day was upon us. He believed our nation was on the brink of destruction; he was right. We were approaching an abyss that required a miracle to prevent us from tipping into.

With his announcement an air of utter disbelief immediately spread across the airwaves of every media outlet. He couldn't be serious! Initially there was laughter and derision, but no inkling of what was to be. This man had contributed to almost every political campaign of significance. Lest he be jesting, they dared not hurl too many insults that first day. Those that remained quiet believed there was a chance still hoped he would contribute to them!

He did not; he was serious.

His announcement was shocking to many. The media had perfected the pursuit of controlling the American people with absolute disinformation. Many had barely noticed that the truth was nowhere to be found in their 'nightly news' broadcasts. The dreaded 'propaganda' of yesteryear was now being served to the people in regular doses daily, nighty, and 24 hours a day through cable news outlets. The newscasters took a pause to get directions from their own 'handlers.' How exactly should they publicly respond to this? The decision had already been made for them.

A rumbling of laughter, jeers and a hint of smears began. In fact, they had already decided their allegiance would be granted to their chosen one, Hillary Clinton. Those who controlled the airwaves never entertained the idea that America had a choice.

A silent war began in America that day.

Initially, the voters were unsure of Donald Trump's plans to lead a nation. He was a completely different candidate!

Although he was in unfamiliar territory, many people felt they truly knew him better than any politician. He was their 'Donald.' Curiosity drove them to his events, in large numbers. For perhaps the first time in our history, lines of people and cars began forming at every appearance for his political events.

Was he serious? Could he help them? His business acumen was undeniable; did that translate to leading their country? The obvious question was why would he? He had exemplified the American Dream, perfected it and was living it. The sum paid to an American President was paltry in his world.

What could prompt him to give that up? He did not need the fame, he had it in spades. He did not need the opportunity for fortune; he had long since amassed billions of dollars. Soon the people realized the only reason he would do this was exactly as he stated. He cared about America, the people, their heritage and their future. This was a brand new American ballgame.

America loves ballgames, the tougher the better.

And so began a battle that would make the movie 'Rocky 4' pale in comparison as we watched a real life battle between good and evil. 'The Donald' had stepped into an arena where there were no officials to call illegal moves, no rules that were written or observed and no hope of a victory… they thought.

Tens of millions of Americans began watching; soon they were cheering for this fighter. The opposition believed he would go down on his knees and surrender, lest he be destroyed; for that was the plan

There were speeches that soon became epic and debates filled with ridicule from the media masses. The American people found them spellbinding. For this was a fighter, tough and relentless. He would box the ears of any who dared challenge him. He literally kicked 16 well known politicians off the stage as he took the center position, the winning position, in each and every debate. Soon the people knew he would not go down easy, if ever. He was still standing, still fighting and still believing he could win.

We watched in awe as he endured their spitefulness and hate filled rhetoric. The roar of their loud cheers pierced the carefully controlled airwaves at every rally and speech. In the midst of those cheers, he still stood strong in the face of unimaginable opposition.

This was a championship ballgame, the toughest we had ever witnessed. The American people were up for the challenge. The cheers had begun, a smattering at first and then the loud roar of solid support. Finally the thunder of the American people who had embraced this man rang loud and clearly as they learned to respect him in a different way.

The Trump mantra of 'winning, winning, winning' took on a whole new life. We watched him not only survive their blows but land punches no one had ever dared to throw. His attackers were the people who identified as the 'elite'. They did so proudly while the people looked on in disgust. They barely noticed the reaction of the American voters they planned to 'serve,' for the people were of little or no consequence to them.

Donald Trump dared to stare straight into the face of evil.

We watched in dismay as his opponent declared she would end hundreds of thousands of job in fossil fuels, jobs that fed and clothed those she was certain would vote for her. She showed no evidence of having noticed their stares of disbelief as she spoke, often down, to them. The American political class had long since left the people and embarked on their own journey that was certain to destroy the very people they purported to serve. Their words made it apparent they felt the people no longer had a choice.

They very nearly didn't; until that famous escalator ride. Most Americans had no idea how far things had descended in their country.

They were frankly horrified as the depths of depravation were exposed. The debates between Hillary Clinton and Donald Trump graphically disclosed her support for late term abortion; right up to the moment of birth.

Americans soon realized their willingness to look away from those many changes over the years had had brought them to the doorstep of utter immorality and evil. They were being asked to support infanticide. How could this righteous and just nation have descended into such depraved thinking? A great shudder spread across our land. How could this have happened; were we not looking?

Like the drip, drip of water on a rock our basic and fundamental moral values had eroded into nothingness.

The contemptuous sneers and jeers from the opposition, many delivered by the media, did not fall on deaf ears. The American people heard them all.

Soon we realized it was no longer safe to honestly express how we felt. For these people were far more dangerous than we had imagined. It was not enough for them to attack a contender, to destroy his life. Suddenly they were attacking the supporters of Donald Trump, dragging them out of cars at stop lights and practicing the Marxist tool of 'Cancel Culture' against every dissenter. The Saul Alinsky playbook had been incorporated into American politics in its ugliest form.

This was war; one that would determine whether 'we the people; would survive and thrive in a nation we had all created, or accept utter defeat and surrender our nation, and all of her glory, to the darkest of concepts, Socialism/Communism.

Every attack was magnified; every person who dared to speak out became fair game. The American people were effectively silenced, expected to do exactly as instructed lest their hateful practices destroy our lives.

A Trojan horse had been allowed into our government. Few Americans truly understood back then how dark these days were.

Before us was the evidence that institutions we had long believed in were corrupt to the core. They were willing to contrive events, fabricate stories of criminal intent, lie to our courts and deceive our people. All of these actions were taken to force us to vote for the candidate they had chosen for us. The corruption was seeping through the pores of once respected people.

And there we stood, with the stench permeating every facet of our lives.

They dared us to stand against them, all the while snickering at the idea that the citizens of America stood a chance against their corruption. They were in charge!

On November 8, 2016 the American people came face to face with a decision not unlike the one our nation had faced once before in our history.

When General George Washington knelt to pray before leading his soldiers, cold, underfed and enormously outgunned to face the most powerful military on the face of the earth he knew he had two choices. He could retreat in defeat and surrender, ensuring they would die as traitors to England, or gather his courage, trust in his Creator and boldly move forward to victory. In the end, there was no choice; it was a victory for liberty or certain death.

Americans were now faced with losing our liberty and the very foundation we stood on as Americans, that of freedom and justice for all. It was a certain future of exceptionalism, or kneeling at the feet of politicians who believed they had become a new class of emperors.

They were certain that the people had given up and accepted their new vision of America. Why wouldn't they be? They had harnessed the very top level of our Intelligence Community to cover their sins and destroy any who dared to oppose them. It was frightening to all who paid close attention to the events unfolding before us.

Far worse, they had commandeered the one protection granted by our Constitution to protect 'We the people,' the free press. It was their duty to find truth and deliver it faithfully to the people. So important was this to protect our freedom they were granted Constitutional protection to ensure their ability to faithfully expose the truth. The guards at the gates of our freedom had defected, leaving those who depended on them fully exposed to the threats these people brought to America's freedom. Their actions could easily allow our nation to fall; yet they agreed.

The DNA of the American citizen is that of standing tall for righteousness, for defending and protecting those who could not protect themselves and for carrying the banner of freedom to a hilltop where the light of that freedom would always be a beacon of hope. These are the values we have fought for and lost many lives to defend. We had laid it all on the line, only to be sold out like rotting produce at a roadside stand at the hands of lying, deceitful, corrupt politicians who were far more dangerous than any military might we have faced.

Somewhere in the midst of all this ugliness the American people stood up, stood tall and made a choice, once again. They determined that this was a price we would not pay, regardless of the consequences. They would go boldly and bravely forward and begin to right these immeasurable wrongs with the simple act of saying 'No, not anymore.' The people rose up, just as they had for General Washington, left their homes, got their weapons and flanked the opposition, not on a battleground like Gettysburg but at the ballot box. Their powerful weapon was the right to vote and to have their choice counted. The stand they took that election cycle changed the face of all Americans tomorrows.

They elected Donald John Trump as the 45th President of The United States of America, determining that their liberty and justice for all must stand and endure.

This was the beginning of those chants, 'We Love YOU!'

And God Blessed America.

2 THE CRACKS BEGIN

On November 9, 2016 shortly after 2:45 AM EST Donald Trump took the stage to give his Victory speech. His wide smile was tinged with humility as he surveyed the large crowd of supporters who had waited through the long night to celebrate with him. He had won!

His infectious spirit of 'Winning Winning Winning' had taken on a whole new meaning; tens of millions of people had joined this mantra.

Against the longest imaginable odds a new leader and a new future had been chosen for America. Finally, at about 2:30 AM EST the final acknowledgement came that Donald Trump had won the 2016 Presidential election. The race could easily have been called by 10:30 PM, but it wasn't.

Those who were charged with making the final call simply refused to believe the results, holding out for the slimmest hope that something was wrong. His winning was impossible!

The final tally of votes in Michigan and Pennsylvania dashed the dying hopes of the naysayers. For them, this was a day in infamy, again.

The viewers who stayed tuned to the broadcasts witnessed tears, anger and utter disbelief by the 'newscasters.' Donald Trump's loss had been a foregone conclusion to the media. Throughout the night they had laughed and jeered at the man who had once been a colleague on many networks. It was impossible for him to win. But he had.

There were cutouts on every station, checking in to hear the forthcoming concession speech of the loser several times. But none was coming that night. The people gathered for her had planned a celebration party of enormous magnitude with $7 million dollars of fireworks to celebrate their win. Instead they stared in disbelief, and cried.

Meanwhile, the streets of New York outside the news networks stations were filling with massive crowds. They were cheering and carrying Trump/Pence signs and flags. The people in these crowds were not surprised. They were elated; they had finally won. It was as simple as going to the voting prescient and casting a ballot; a cherished right our founding fathers knew could protect us all.

The veil of darkness that had descended upon America decades before began to part early on November 9, 2016. The cracks in our society were enormous, as seen by the continuing disbelief of the media who could hardly accept this outcome.

For them, years of grieving began that night.

One has to wonder if they had ever considered how their country had been changing, or what those changes could mean to their own lives. They had blindly accepted that the planned changes were great and they would be the beneficiaries of a transformed nation. The truth was much darker. They were just pawns moved about at will in a massive scheme to capture and destroy the very soul of America.

The cracks formed that night were necessary; a change of course was being set into motion.

The government of the United States of America is the biggest business in the word. The biggest ship on the planet had altered course and was making a wide turn back to its home port. A dramatic change of course must cause cracks in the plans of powerful people, those plans that had gone awry in this election.

Yet through the cracks, the healing begins. Light was slowly streaming in those cracks that night.

Unbeknown to the millions of Americans who chose to make a change in that historic election, those who chose to march to the ballot box and stand for their country, their actions had overturned plans so profound they rippled across the globe.

The emotion that inspired Francis Scott Key in 1814 to compose 'The Star Spangled Banner' sprang to life in the march of the people to the ballot box on November 8, 2016.

For a Trump loss on November 8th 2016 would have left many crying out, "Oh, say does that star spangled banner still wave,' necessary to ask as our country would no longer be recognizable. It was doubtful the things our nation has long stood for could have withstood the onslaught of changes planned for America had the other candidate won.

This was a historic election, one that changed the face of a nation.

3 A CHARISMATIC LEADER EMERGES

As the world attempted to make sense of the astounding results of the November 8, 2016 election the stock market lurched and then surged forward. If you are 'tuned in' to energy you may have heard the whine and roar as the engine of the American economy sprang to life.

Not since Ronald Reagan, who followed the dismal performance of Jimmy Carter, had the pulse of the US economy been felt so strongly. Businesses, whose life blood depended on a President who understood the economy, breathed a sigh of relief. For them, the past many years could be likened to being a terminal patient. By 2016 many expected their business to die. Not since Ronald Reagan had there been a President friendly to the growth of small business, the life blood of our economy.

The housing industry has always been a leading indicator of our economy.

Six in ten jobs originate from the housing industry. This includes the road builders, surveyors, every trade contractor involved in new construction and remodeling, all the county jobs required to meet codes and filing of documents, landscapers, painters, realtors and bankers. Add to that the surveyors, mortgage bans, realtors and title agencies. Walk through your home and look around you. Everything that exists in the construction and maintenance of it is part of that 6 out of 10. Don't forget the truckers who hauled the materials, those who hauled gas to the stations for the workers to purchase on the way to the new jobs and the manufacturing jobs to create all the materials. Then you get a better understanding of how housing and new construction affects our jobs market and the economy.

Why does this matter in President Trump's election? Our President is a builder, it is oh, so important! He understands business, construction and hard work. It was a new day in America. We no longer had a politician who owed every big supporter a favor, one who could never carry out their promises to us. We had a solid businessman with a proven track record. Even more, his business transactions had taken him abroad to many other nations to build businesses that affected their economy. He already understood their needs and knew how to work with them.

In the midst of all the newscasters talk about his lack of experience, Donald Trump may very well have entered the position of President with more experience that mattered than any who came before him.

He understood the stock market with all its intricacies and how it affected every American who had a pension fund or 401K. Donald Trump understood how every facet of the American economy worked, what could never work and what must be done to build a strong and lasting economy.

There may be others who understand these things as well. Yet, to know, to understand and to execute the changes was not nearly enough.

To beat those sixteen people on stage and then to tackle an opponent the American people knew very well seemed impossible. He ran against a person most believed was entitled to win; many had not believed she could be beaten.

Donald Trump was not just any opponent while he was not a politician, he was a man most Americans had willingly invited into their living rooms once a week for many years. He was an enigma long before he was our President. He was 'The Donald!' That was a powerful position.

'The Donald' stood apart from just any man; he exuded confidence, wit, humor and intelligence. He had suffered great losses on the road to his enormous successes. Somehow he gathered the bits and pieces of those losses and rolled them into a new idea that would win far bigger than the lost project could ever have become.

'No' has never meant 'No' to this man; it has simply meant 'not that way.'

When things got tough and seemed to go badly he stepped outside of that mind set and dared to dream even bigger.

Why not? His favorite line is, 'What do you have to lose?' He loved the pursuit to a new win and was fearless in the fight. If it appeared he had been knocked down he seemed oblivious to the idea. "The Donald' had already looked ahead and realized what he could gain from the last misstep. He has the mind of a champion.

There was never a time when Donald Trump believed he would be given the election. He had been acutely aware that hard work and perseverance was required to realize the mantra of 'winning, winning, winning' he was famous for. And work he did. The last day before the election found him crisscrossing the nation in his now famous 'Trump' plane for 6 rallies. The final one wrapped up well into Election Day.

That alone is remarkable but not the most surprising thing. Thousands of people trudged down a frozen dirt road to nowhere to find their way to the small airport where Donald Trump was holding his final rally in Michigan. It was well after midnight; dark, windy and cold… and packed with thousands of people. This man brought hope to millions of people who were ready to give up on the dream of a bright future. They instinctively knew he loved the country as much as they did. They were hungry for hope.

In spite of all of this, it still was not enough to win a very corrupt American election. It required so much more; something that could not be bought or bartered for.

The magic that propelled Donald Trump into the winners circle was the stardust of charisma.

Less than 2% of the world population is blessed with this gift. When you encounter it in any person at some deep level you understand that person was born to do something big. Remember President Ronald Reagan's remark years earlier when he shook Donald Trump's hand and commented, 'I feel like I'm shaking the hand of a future President.' The lives of charismatic people leave a lasting impression on everyone who comes into contact with them; they remember meeting them, and the details around that meeting for years to come.

Ronald Reagan and John F. Kennedy enjoyed this kind of charisma. Regardless of whether one agreed with their political positions, people were drawn to them to hear speeches and in personal appearances. They left an unforgettable impression. Frequently their words are embedded into our memory.

Princess Diana of Wales is another example of this kind of charisma. The public could never get enough of reading about her and watching her life. We were at some deep level drawn to watch the most mundane events.

There is yet another trait charismatic people share that is ever so endearing.

They are caring, many times brutally honest and wear their hearts on their sleeves. They exude things that most people need; like understanding, compassion and empathy. They instinctively take the time to listen to others and really care about ways they might be able to help them.

Donald Trump has been quietly helping people for decades. When a need arose he put on his hard hat, called for his workers and jumped in to fix what was broken. When those measures were not required, he wrote a check and wished them well.

He is a born mover and shaker. This is another trait charisma embraces as it becomes embedded in the very few and chosen people who are blessed to have it.

Donald Trump was blessed with that gift. He was on the scene of American politics for a reason. The people responded to him, trusted him and prayed he could deliver. And he did.

4 A RISING TIDE

President John F. Kennedy introduced Americans to the concept of 'A rising tide lifts all boats.' Those of us who paid attention to the economy lived the effects of that concept. It literally means that a good economy provides opportunity for everyone and is essential to lifting people from poverty to hope, providing new prospects for a better future. This concept defines the American Dream.

Donald Trump grew up in Queens, NY. It was a place ripe with opportunity for those who had a good strong work ethic, people like his father. While his father was very successful in the real estate industry he insisted on good work ethics, never allowing his children to fall into the trap of entitlement. This is the foundation of the man elected as the 45th President of the Unite States. Donald Trump is a tireless worker who still expects to work hard to achieve his goals.

Hard work began in his childhood, following through his formative years. College offered more opportunities to excel academically and in sports. Shortly after graduating from Wharton School of Business he assumed the leadership of his father's business.

He promptly renamed it 'The Trump Organization.' This act was a small window into how he thinks. An organization does not embody one person, but rather the efforts of many. All the way back to 1971 it became apparent that Donald Trump would become the undisputed leader of a winning team. He planned it that way.

He laid down a foundation for everyone to succeed and be recognized for their successes. A quick scan of the numerous video clips when Donald Trump was the speaker at any event began with him thanking several different people by name. That trait continues today.

He always recognizes the efforts of others and how they contributed to a successful project he is addressing. In the face of strong opposition to his style, he has always combined excellent manners with a very brash presentation. He is a fighter who intends to win.

We see this regularly in press briefings as he faces an incredibly hostile press. He calls on each reporter by simply saying, 'please.' They are given a polite opening and allowed to respond in the manner they choose. Typically it is with hostility; this invites the brash and unpolished responses he has become famous for.

While previous presidents would silently seethe, President Trump quickly exposes the very things no one has dared to speak about. The press and the public found it shocking. There are always immediate efforts to discredit and ridicule him. The passing of time has proven he was 100% accurate in his assessment.

Donald Trump is a pragmatic visionary, two qualities not typically found together. He understands what is possible and very likely knows how to make those things a reality. He has little if any time for pretense. If it is a duck before him he prefers to quickly identify it and call it out.

This has made the inner circle of Washington DC horribly uncomfortable.

These people have existed in a bubble of corruption the likes of which the American people had never even imagined. They had no intention of allowing him to penetrate and certainly never to remain in their circle. He simply had to go, the sooner the better. But he refused.

The newspaper headlines and daily network news were glaring in their condemnation of this new President. With wanton abandon and willfulness they freely lied to the nation in their efforts to make him run away before they completely destroyed him and his family. He refused.

There is little doubt that the Trump family was shocked at the viciousness of these attacks, at the extreme efforts made to destroy each and every member of the family. Ten year old Barron did not escape their contempt.

Gradually a dawning realization of the depths America had fallen into became crystal clear to he citizens. When the attacks began, mostly about his business dealings, the persistent chants of Russia, Russia, Russia and the corruption that was slowly emerging, it was not lost on the American people. Many Americans took a long pause and attempted to learn what was going on.

We thought we had seen the depths the media had sunken to, but a brand new level of vitriol emerged. Initially it was difficult to imagine the newscasters we had once trusted were intentionally lying to their viewers; not in America!

Yet systematically, investigation after investigation led to nothing at all.

For many it took three years of the contrived, relentless attacks for them to realize there was some grand scheme afoot in our country. That 'something' was pulsating with evil.

If the American people had become complacent during this time, Donald Trump had not. It appeared he had dedicated a few hours every day to put on his fireman's hat and extinguish their new flames of lies and destruction. Then he headed straight back to his office, rolled up his sleeves and pressed forward with his famous work ethic.

He had much to accomplish if he were to save the nation he loved. Donald Trump had less and less time to be caught in their web of lies. He had an innate understanding that if he were to lift the people who had entrusted him with this power to a better place, a monumental task lay ahead.

5 THE GATES UNGUARDED

Constitution of United States of America 1789 (rev. 1992)
Amendment 1

'Congress shall make no law respecting an establishment of religion, or prohibiting the free exercise thereof; or abridging the freedom of speech, **or of the press**; or the right of the people peaceably to assemble, and to petition the Government for a redress of grievances.'

Our Founding Fathers were brilliant by most assessments. This is likely the result of the experience they had gained by living under the rule of a monarchy with a very clear caste system. They went to great lengths to protect this new idea of a Republic where the people were more powerful than the government. Within this new concept lay the opportunity for personal freedom and the right to thrive.

The goal was truly liberty and justice, equally, for all.

Few Americans today have taken the time to really look at the battles that were fought and how truly fraught with peril it had been for those who dared to build a new nation, declaring their independence.

The writings and songs from that period use the words 'perilous' repeatedly, because it was. It took a monumental act of courage to stand against the most powerful military might on the planet with so little to fight the battle with. Had they lost, their heads would have been placed on London Bridge for all to see what happens to those who dare to flee.

This was powerful inspiration for the bedraggled, cold and hungry army of the 13 American Colonies. It was a fledgling new nation born from a wilderness that was fairly untamed; yet filled with determination and pride in their new concept. It would later be called the greatest experiment in the history of mankind. Only the strong could survive this quest.

The founders knew the groundwork for governance had to be laid, but it was not a simple task. Even in the beginning, when freedom of expression was barely more than an idea, those who came to the meeting of the Continental Congress to hammer out the constitution had their own ideas.

They were incredibly wary of giving too much power to this new government. It was essential that the states remained sovereign and able to set their own course while they crafted a Federal Government that could adequately protect their citizens from all threats, foreign and domestic.

From 1774 to 1789, the 13 American colonies which later became the United States were served by The Continental Congress, serving as their governing body. In 1775, the Second Continental Congress convened after the American Revolutionary War had already begun.

In 1776, the Congress took the profound step of declaring America's independence from Britain. It would be five years before Congress ratified the first national constitution, the Articles of Confederation. Our nation was governed under these Articles until 1789, when it was replaced by the current United States Constitution.

Congress was designed with emphasis on the equality of the citizens, intending to promote free debate. After a lengthy and sometimes very heated discussion, Congress finally issued a Declaration of Rights.
James Madison drafted most of the Bill of Rights. He was a Virginia representative who would later become the fourth president of the United States. Madison was an attorney at law who had many times defended others against tyranny. He understood all too well how government must be constrained to protect the rights of the people in the new Republic.

All of the Founders agreed that the governing documents must be strong enough to grant the necessary powers to secure the foundation yet still provide a method of checks and balances to protect the people. They also understood that some method must be in place to inform the citizens, to provide truthful and unbiased information to the people. It was necessary to provide this information in order for the people to clearly see what events were shaping the nation and more importantly, how the leaders planned to govern them. Their freedom was of the utmost importance. They had fought battles and wars to create a new free nation of the people, by the people and for the people. It must be protected from within by the people.

That search for a 'guard at the gates of freedom' led to the inclusion of the words, **'or the press'** in the first amendment to our Constitution. They were granted this protection for the sole purpose of providing accurate and unbiased information to the citizens, allowing them to make a free choice for their nation's future in elections. The press was granted the same protection as a citizen of the nation. This protection rendered them the sentinels of protecting the free exchange of ideas in the United States of America. Their duty was to stand guard at the gates of our freedom.

Sometime in the mid 1960's a coalition of people formed quietly in the background. By the year 2020 they would famously become known as 'the Deep State.' Their goals were insidious, their planning meticulous. This groups intentions would have, at the time of nations founding, been considered treasonous. For obvious reasons, they maintained a tight knit alliance that was well hidden from the public eye.

Their agenda was slowly creeping into the society of America. The race riots and turmoil in the 1960's were just the beginning, a practice run to see what the people would accept.

At the same time they began infiltrating our schools; academia took on a whole new look. History books were destroyed and replaced with information that no longer told the real stories of the extraordinary people who had built our country. Education was slowly gravitating to a place where the children were taught that their nation's history was shameful. Nothing could be farther than the truth. While not a perfect nation, efforts would always continue to a more perfect Union of ideas and the betterment of this new society.

Indoctrination replaced education. Gradually, the children were taught what to think rather than how to think and debate their own ideas. This is an insidious practice typically found in Communist nations. Most Americans did not know that a ground level rot had taken hold; it was growing in the foundation of their country with the capability of destroying it.

The practices that would lead to the acceptance of Socialism and Communism were gradually introduced to America, like water dripping onto a rock; they ever so quietly became acceptable conversation. These ideas began to erode the moral values in this magnificent pillar of freedom.

Ronald Reagan encountered this hostility as he ran for and won an election to become the 40th president of the United States in 1980. He became a highly influential voice of modern conservatism. It was about that time that we began to suspect that our news organizations were biased and left leaning. They had already begun to act as an arm of the Democratic Party.

News organizations began to change rather quickly after that, most notably when cable news was introduced. Those with ill intentions were provided a 24 hour a day platform to subvert the lasting ideals of America.
They were later purchased by wealthy entrepreneurs and organizations that held deep politically biased views. They became an important part of the "Deep State.' Soon they were firmly in control of the 'news' America would be given. They were vicious and brutal in their assault on any organization or person who dared to contradict them. They had a mission, an evil one that could destroy our Republic. Their intention was to transform this nation into one where exceptionalism would become a thing of the past.

Today 6 entities control the content of the bulk of the news the American people are offered. All are far left liberals. Propaganda has replaced trusted news in our country. Beyond those organizations it is necessary to search online or live streaming new groups for unbiased news.

These are the people who ordered the guards at our gates of freedom to abandon their post. This is the source of the vitriol that Donald Trump, an outsider who certainly could see through their plan encountered in a brutal manner.

More than any other issue facing America and her citizens today, this is the most dangerous to the future of the country. It is the soil where the ground rot grows. The intent is to destroy everything our Founders fought for and created. Donald Trump recognized this and had no intention of allowing it to happen, if only the American people would stand behind him and fight. And they did.

6 A NEW DAY DAWNS

On January 20, 2017 Donald John Trump was sworn in as the 45th President of the United States of America. More than 60 million Americans breathed a sigh of relief. For them, the past sixteen years had been a rough roller coaster ride. They never wanted to look back.

For the rest of the voters, those whose candidate had lost, they began initiating a treacherous plan that had been crafted very carefully by the same 'Deep State' who now commanded the formerly free press.

After lengthy investigations we have learned that less than a week after the election of 2016 this group held a meeting in NY City. They numbered more than one hundred, the wealthiest and most powerful on earth. 'No' was an unfamiliar term to them in any fashion. They believed themselves to be so powerful they would chart a new course for an entire nation of people now numbering nearly 330 million. They held no regard whatsoever for those people. They may yet prove to be as powerful as they imagine.

These people had no intention of accepting Donald Trump as president. It appears to have never occurred to them that they had no right to subvert the will of tens of millions of American people.

Years and years of planning had gone into the position they held at the time of that election. They were ever so close to bringing America to her knees. There would be little opportunity for the nation to ever rise again.

Donald Trump was not a player; he refused to be a part of their plan or to allow them to implement their new ideas into a nation he loved. More than anyone, it is likely that the new president knew exactly what was planned, and who was behind it. He was very familiar with this group and their goals.

That he knew and understood their plan made him more dangerous than most. When you know the elements and the rules of a different playbook, you understand what has to be removed to topple the foundation. Donald Trump did know; this makes it obvious why they believed he must be removed at all costs. More than half a century of careful planning and execution had suddenly been upended by 'We the people.' It was unacceptable. The *'resistance'* was born.

It consisted of a brutal regime including the top levels of intelligence in America; the National Intelligence Agency, the Central Intelligence Agency, the Federal Bureau of Investigation, the National Security Council, Some members of the Secret Service, the Industrial Complex, (a military giant) the news media, unlimited funding, secret military participation and those wealthy billionaires that had met in NY. It also included a legion of former and current politicians who had benefitted from and were sworn to protect this group of elite anarchists who had spent years working to transform America into a Socialist/Communist nation.

The American people recognized the politicians as their names spewed forth; they included the intelligence top brass and many others. It was shocking to see them fall one by one. That they were able to be toppled defied any explanation when one examines the power that was protecting them. Perhaps the guiltiest of these is the news media whose job it was to protect the people of the nation. They had become co-conspirators.

It is an accepted fact that if you are able to support a viewpoint for 60 days consecutively you will have accomplished indoctrination of those who listen to you. This had been going on for years. Much of America had been effectively brain washed with the tactics employed by the media.

The hostile and criminal treatment of Donald Trump, his candidacy and his presidency would take years to uncover. It was never intended to be known.

Those who had voted for him knew they had taken a risk. He was an unknown in the political arena. It was necessary to trust deeply to hand over the reins of ones future. There was some slight skepticism, likely fueled by the jeers and taunts of the press. But at least in this new leader there was hope; it was something that had been trampled on in the past many years. America had been betrayed. Those who chose Donald Trump knew the end of the nation they loved was near unless they dared to do something different.

It was more than uncomfortable to watch the maneuvers of the FBI, CIA and NIA as they worked hard to diminish this new leader. These were people we had grown to trust over a long period of time. It was unimaginable that they were at the core of such corruption.

One insidious plan after another emerged, like sewage seeping through the cracks in the floor. Those we once trusted were exposed; they appeared as the worst kind of villains in a Batman movie. The Joker was truly wild now, multiplying by the day.

Many supporters of the new president were dismayed by the news of General Flynn, the National Security Advisor, leaving the Administration.

Just as had been planned by the opposition, we wondered if we had made a mistake in our judgement. He was close to Donald Trump and was suddenly portrayed as corrupt. He left the White House and we waited to see where the next event might take us. It was all too sobering and difficult to understand.

The supporters who had been riding the wave of positive energy introduced by Donald Trump and his win sat with baited breath, listening to the daily and sometimes hourly reports against the new administration. Every cabinet appointment brought a new wave of heated debate about the member's inadequate background, corrupt ideas and incompetence for the job. Not a single person was excluded from the jeers and taunts that had now become the normal on our nightly news.

Many Americans grew weary of this quickly. There was a fundamental rule of human nature that had been ignored by the 'Deep State' in their plans.

Negativity, rage and fear drive people away. They served it up hourly; it quickly became a blur of bad news we no longer wanted to hear. It was far easier to simply change the channel or turn off the TV and wait to see what happened. Most found it pretty nauseating.

It is very telling that about that same time Yogi Bear and Boo Boo's 50 year old antics were more watched then most of the news programs. The American people had truly had enough. Theirs is not a society based on negativity. They are a 'can do' kind of people who look for and find solutions and move on. This is the DNA of Americans.

It is an understatement to suggest that the people of the nation began to suspect that something was amiss in the news. We were beginning to see positive results of a Trump Administration, all the while being treated to a daily dose of more negative news.

It is difficult to imagine what our new President was enduring throughout all of these unwarranted and brutal assaults. He and his family were mercilessly attacked. Everyone around him, including his supporters came under attack. To trust anyone was fraught with peril. One can imagine that the founders experienced this very conundrum when they decided to form their own country. The word peril was once again introduced into American politics. It's a powerful word when it describes a time in place in your own life.

We witnessed a quick succession of changes with very, very few people in the media who were willing to honestly address what was happening. Sean Hannity of Fox news was probably the first to openly examine the facts and deliver them to the people. These same 'Deep State' players immediately attempted to cancel his show. The truth was beyond shocking; America was far closer to the brink than we had ever suspected.

In short succession, and in the fiery manner for which Donald Trump had become famous, James Comey, the FBI director was fired, followed by the exit of Reince Priebus, White House Chief of Staff, Anthony Scaramucci, White House Communications Director and Tom Price, Health and Human Services Director. All had the shortest service in the history of their positions respectively.

Our heads were spinning with the exits and the major news those exits created. As the truth emerged, their leaving was the right actions to protect America, Donald Trump and his Presidency. As the investigations moved forward, James Comey was believed by many to be the leader in the pack of 'Deep State' corruption that was revealed.

While a new day had dawned in America when Donald Trump assumed the Presidency, hurricane force winds were swirling around this new administration. It was called 'Crossfire Hurricane,' a sinister plan to remove the new president. There were no limits or boundaries this group would not penetrate in their efforts to remove and destroy Donald Trump.

Even after those revelations and exits, it wasn't over. Lo, it had just begun. There was so much more to come for the United States of America and Donald Trump.

7 EXTREME JUSTICE

On February 13, 2016 Supreme Court Justice Antonin Scalia died. He was considered by many to be the most prominent voice of conservatism on the court. His uncompromising decisions were always strict interpretations of the constitution as it was written. He refused to stray from what he believed was the purpose of the court. Antonin Scalia was a beloved voice for conservative Americans; his death was widely mourned.

Scalia's death presented a golden opportunity to far left liberals. President Obama was leaving office, but there was still time to nominate and confirm a new left leaning Justice. Judge Merrick Garland was quickly chosen to fill the vacancy.

Unfortunately for them, the Republicans had control of the Senate. In order to move him forward to confirmation, it was necessary for the Senate Majority leader, Mitch McConnell to schedule the required hearings and the vote to confirm Merrick. He refused to do so.

His refusal was not nearly as outrageous as the fuming liberals claimed. In fact, twenty nine times in our country's history a vacancy has become available on the Supreme Court in an election year. In every instance the president made a nomination to fill the vacancy. Twenty times in our country's history the party of the President and the Senate were in control when a vacancy opened. The confirmation did go forward in all but two. One involved Abraham Lincoln's appointment. The Senate was not in session when a Justice Salmon P. Chase died. It was not possible to gather the Senators and bring them back into session before the election. It was 1873; travel and communications were severely limited compared to today's standards. This was grossly misrepresented by Vice Presidential nominee Kamala Harris in her debate with Vice President Mike Pence. When the Presidency and Senate majority are not of the same party, the nomination has only gone forward to confirmation twice in an election year in our history.

McConnell's failure to even schedule the hearings was an unforgivable affront to the Democrat Party. They would likely never let it be forgotten, even though a result of no confirmation was by far the normal in that same circumstance in our history.

Candidate Donald Trump knew filling the vacancy was incredibly important to the country. Regardless of one's political position, the seat mattered to America. He released a list of more than 20 viable people to fill the vacancy and promised to choose from that list if elected. It was the first time this had ever happened.

Conservatives across the nation considered this to be one of the most important issues in selecting a new leader. They had no way of knowing if Donald Trump would honor his promise to choose from the list, but all acknowledged that the list contained qualified and acceptable names. Millions decided to take a chance and vote for the Trump/Pence ticket.

If you closely examine how Donald Trump handled this process you are able to gain a small insight into the methods he operates to gain success in making deals; the kind that led to writing his book, 'The Art of the Deal.' When Trump identifies any issue that could potentially break a deal he addresses it before the deal is on the table. This eliminates a potential stumbling block in the path of success. It is a bold move but one he has habitually employed, and continued throughout his first 4 years in office.

Donald Trump honored that promise after he was elected, choosing Neil Gorsuch as the person to fill the seat vacated by Scalia. The Democrats were not happy but there was little they could do; he was confirmed in a fairly contentious battle in the Senate.

And then, Justice Anthony Kennedy, a strong conservative voice on the court, retired. Donald Trump appointed Judge Brett Kavanaugh to fill the seat. There were no viable reasons not to confirm him to the position; he was well qualified and an excellent candidate.

Unfortunately what unfolded in the attempt by the Democrats to block his confirmation set a new record in ugliness by the US Senate. He was smeared in a way the citizens of America had never witnessed. Kavanaugh was brutally attacked with statements that would quickly prove to be untrue. Most Americans were appalled by the scene that played out in that hearing.

A full blown hate filled and vitriolic circus under the guise of a hearing unfolded before the American people. The media went into overdrive in their blatant attacks of him at every level. We had never witnessed this kind of smear in our political arena. The McCarthy trials may have been a close second but this was a brand new level of contempt for the people and the institution. Kavanaugh was eventually confirmed but not without substantial damage to the ideals America had grown accustomed to. We were embarrassed for the Senate while feeling great compassion for Kavanaugh and his family, who attended the hearings.

By that time, America had become a brand new landscape. It would prove to be nothing compared to the years that lay ahead. With respect to the Supreme Court, the unimaginable happened just before the 2020 election.

Ruth Bader Ginsburg, the lioness of the liberal party on the Supreme Court, died. Her death was not really unexpected as she had several bouts with cancer, but the timing could not have been worse for Democrat's. A new seat had opened on the Supreme Court, again. The angst that had been on display for Justice Kavanaugh's confirmation roared back to life.

The Democrats and far left liberals went into overdrive with their predictions of the doom and gloom that awaited America if Donald Trump were permitted to appoint a third justice to the court. The media and Democrats railed at the very idea. Their rhetoric ranged from a hatred of all things Trump to any appointment being illegitimate. In truth, they had always considered Trump to be an illegitimate president simply because they said so. Their rage knew no bounds.

Six days later President Donald Trump appointed Judge Amy Coney Barrett to fill the seat. Barrett was perhaps the role model for a candidate to the court. She had been through the process of being confirmed to the Federal Appeals Court a scant two years before. The Senators knew her, knew her record and had more than one hundred of her new decisions to review in this new confirmation hearing. None believed there was any smoking gun that could derail the confirmation.

The level of hateful rhetoric expressed in the previous Kavanaugh selection paled in comparison. Oddly enough, this time the attacks were aimed at the President who was required by the Constitution to make an appointment. It is possible that the Democrat Senators remembered how badly their treatment of Kavanaugh had been received by the American people. It was very close to the election of 2020, leaving little time to repair any damage they caused.

President Trump followed the same precedent that every president before him had, yet Trump was excoriated for doing so. They were oh, so angry.

Mitch McConnell was equally attacked as he made the decision to go forward with the confirmation hearings; again the same process that was followed 20 times before his decision in our country. Protestors chowed up in front of his home and threatened to burn it down.

President Trump held the news conference announcing the appointment in the Rose Garden of the White House. It became a Republican event by virtue of the Democrats refusal to participate. Shortly thereafter President Trump, the first lady Melania Trump and ultimately thirty six White House workers were diagnosed as positive with Covid 19. All were Republicans.

That too was apparently a Republican event. What followed was an amazing recovery for the president and all of the people infected. President Trump was hospitalized for 3 days and treated with the same antibodies and therapeutics he had been discussing with the public for weeks.

It is fair to say that none of the media outlets expected his recovery to be so quick, if at all. Daily the President released short videos of himself at Walter Reed Medical Center, working as always. He was ever present, but so was something else.

The streets in front of the Medical Center were full of Trump supporters, Trump flags, American flags, baked goods and media. A continuing succession of cars streamed past the supporters. They joined in, blowing horns and cheering for President Trump. Many supporters camped out and never left. There was singing, cheering and prayers for the entire time he was in the hospital. It was not uncommon for them to break out into the chants of 'We love you.' The phenomena of Donald Trump continued. As the number of supporters grew; the chants grew louder. They refused to be silenced. Many said their president could not attend the rallies so they had brought the rallies to him.

President Trump later remarked that he could hear his supporters cheering from the hospital and knew their numbers were great. He made a surprise visit in the back of a Secret Service vehicle to let his supporters know he was aware of and appreciated them. Loud cheers erupted as he drove past waving at his supporters.

That this was an extraordinary event was an understatement.

The chants of 'We love you' had begun about a month prior to this event at the President's 'peaceful protest' rally in North Carolina. Before that happened, there are no recorded events in American history of the public chanting 'We love you' to a President.

The chants only grew louder and more frequent as he fought to recover from the deadly Covid -19 virus. Donald Trump's supporters were faced with the idea of losing his leadership; it was frankly terrifying to many of them. When he left, they believed hope for a normal American future would leave with him. It was very sobering.

Meanwhile, preparations moved forward to confirm his 3rd Justice nominee to the Supreme Court; another record in history was broken.

The war against President Trump raged on. The fury of the Democrat liberals and the media was evident in their refusal at first to believe he really had the virus and finally an attempt to discredit his healing.

This was the new America.

8 THE PRICE OF 'PARXIT"

The Pairs Accord was a treaty that President Obama had helped negotiate and agreed the US would enter into. It was also an agreement that President Trump knew was dangerous for America. There were a lot of things about the Paris Agreement that most Americans knew nothing about. It was introduced to Americans as a 'Global Climate Control Agreement' in a manner that suggested we must support it or be guilty of harming our planet.

One of the most noteworthy requirements of the Paris treaty for fully developed countries like the United States was that it forced the members to make large yearly contributions to the fund. The US was expected to make payments for 10 years before any meaningful payment or action was required from the most significant polluters' on the planet. President Obama originally pledged $3 billion, although future annual contributions would have clearly increased with time; not by a little, by a lot.

There are many good reasons why the Paris Accord was not a good idea for America.

Billions of American tax dollars would have been allocated to members by an institute that operates with very little transparency and accountability. Serious issues had been raised about their corruption over the past 5 years. Those issues were intensified by supporters of the UN climate agenda.

Even worse was the Green Climate Fund's projects involvement in an age old problem where international development money had been systematically diverted by corrupt government officials to other nations.

A Cato Institute representative publicly called it a "slush fund for the world's dictators." He wrote that "Third World tyrants salivate at the prospect of receiving largesse from the green climate fund."

The Paris Agreement was written to accompany the Obama administration's domestic energy agenda, with each bolstering the other. In order to meet our country's "nationally determined contribution" we would have been required to implement domestic policy changes like the Clean Power Plan. This would have made coal, oil, and natural gas considerably more expensive, while subsidizing already expensive energy sources like solar and wind.

Americans would have experienced those increased energy prices throughout the economy. The obvious increases were in utility bills and at the gas pump. It extended to the prices of everyday goods of all kinds to supplement the cost of transporting those products. Obama had promised very early into his first administration that under his plan "electricity rates would necessarily skyrocket."

US compliance with the Paris Accord would have imposed a significantly unequal burden and cost on American industry, comparative to other countries that are much greater emitters of carbon dioxide. Nations like China, India and Russia far exceed the current levels of emission of the USA. In testimony before the House Committee on Science, Space, & Technology in 2016, Stephen Eule of the Institute for 21st Century Energy stated in his testimony, "It is well understood that America's abundance of affordable, reliable energy provides businesses a critical operating advantage in today's intensely competitive global economy. International Energy Agency data reflects a huge comparative energy advantage in natural gas, electricity, and coal prices for U.S. industry compared to its OECD competitors. Prices for these same energy sources in the United States would be two to four times more under this plan."

The Obama administrations domestic energy output was restricted; it embraced activist mantras against fossil fuel production. Under the Trump administration that ideology was reversed. Under the policies of the Trump Administration the US has now surpassed Russia to become the world's largest oil producer and has overtaken Saudi Arabia to become the world's biggest oil exporter. Our natural gas production is number one in the world today. The US has for the first time in 75 years become an energy exporter. These achievements were impossible under an Obama energy policy and the Paris restrictions.

The Obama administration presented the Paris Climate Agreement as something other than a treaty, even though it clearly qualified. As a treaty, the White House would have been required to submit it to the Senate for ratification. This was required by the Constitution; hence they attempted to treat it as something other than a treaty.

They appeared to believe 'it's not a treaty if we say it's not.' This would set a dangerous precedent that could easily topple the balance of powers in our country. It could also give the green light to future presidents to bind the American people to huge financial responsibilities without Congressional oversight and approval, creating a loss of American sovereignty without accountability.

Against enormous opposition, President Trump withdrew from the treaty.

The reality was there was nothing beneficial to the American people in the treaty. It was certain to drive energy costs to new heights and send our remaining manufacturing jobs to nations like China, Mexico and Germany.

Those and many other countries were given as much as 10 years before any restrictions began to apply to them. All were far greater polluters than the US. Looking back, it seems certain that this was yet another lynch pin in the globalist ideal of leveling the playing field, ensuring that American exceptionalism would become a thing of the past.

Politicians in America had spent more than half a century plodding towards a ruinous future for the nation. They had routinely sold out the taxpayers for support of their own futures or to pander to those who had paid their way in elections. The American people had no idea how utterly corrupt their leaders had become. For many, our Constitution was merely a piece of paper they intended to ignore, change or destroy.

Activists gained a firm foothold in the Democrat Party under Obama's tenure as President. The proposals they put forth in many cases violated the restriction of freedoms in the US Constitution. In order to ignore or alter the Constitution, it would be necessary to control the Courts in America both at the state and federal appellate level. These are the courts where Americans can take their grievances and be heard by an impartial third party who can correct the outcome by applying the rules established in the Constitution and Bill of Rights.

It is inexplicable why President Obama more than 100 federal judicial seats open. Most surmise he wanted to allow Hillary Clinton to fill them, never imagining that Donald Trump would win. His win and Mitch McConnell's persistence allowed Donald Trump to fill those lifetime appointment vacancies.

Knowing this, it is easier to understand why the Justices confirmed to the Supreme Court are so important to the globalist's whose views many consider could destroy the America we know and love.

The final lynch pin in this ages old plan is controlling the kinds of nominees confirmed to serve on the Supreme Court. This is the highest court in the land and the final stopping point where the law of the land can be subverted or altered to support a Socialist/Communist future.

Leaving the Paris accord exacerbated the hatred from the far left liberals and those mega billionaires who had attended the meeting in NY City shortly after Donald Trump was elected. Their rage was unleashed in full force on the President and anyone who supported him. It was the beginning of the worst events we had ever witnessed in our country.

The President's supporters felt it was in their best interests to leave the

Paris Accord. They had no desire to volunteer their jobs and tax dollars to the very flawed idea. Most were shocked at the vitriol unleased by the Democrats in power. Their message was carried loudly on every media platform. Every supporter of the President's action was portrayed in an ugly and undesirable manner. Many suggested that they be stalked and confronted at 'gasoline stations, in restaurants, in shopping malls, wherever you see them, get in their face …'

No one in modern history had been a victim of these tactics, and certainly had not encountered such actions before; until those instructions were given to the activists. The hatred of those in power was turned in full force on Trump supporters. Soon these events were so common they were no longer newsworthy.

This was to become the price of 'Parxit.' Americans would all pay.

9 THE WITCHES BREW

witch-hunt /ˈwiCH ˌhənt/ Noun
INFORMAL (meaning)
A campaign directed against a person or group holding unorthodox or unpopular views. ~ Oxford Languages

A strange word emerged into American Politics. 'Witch-hunt;' there it was emerging with the same vengeance we read about with the Salem Witches way back in 1692.

The most ardent of the Trump supporters recoiled for a moment; that word seemed farfetched for a president to use. But President Trump did use it, over and over. What did this mean? What was going on?

The presidency of the United States of America is probably the most serious and far reaching job on earth. It is considered across the globe to be the most powerful position to hold. Before Donald Trump's election it was unthinkable for anyone to imagine they were so powerful they could mount something like a witch-hunt against an American president. That was before we understood the level of arrogance that existed in Washington D.C., our nation's capital.

A fairly large group of unelected bureaucrats, along with several elected congressmen and women combined with some of the most wealthy and powerful citizens and laid the groundwork to remove a duly elected President. This was not a game to them; it was war. They would pull out every stop to win their declared war.

The rumblings of the 'Russia story had already begun; it was a steady drumbeat in the background. Every Executive Order was challenged with a lawsuit to stop any action the President signed. The Justice Department proved to have people within who was a part of this same group. While it was their job to defend the lawsuits and bring order to chaos, we soon learned that some were equally busy mounting charges against the Chief Executive Officer.

There were planted stories and leaks from almost every faction. Legal proceedings ensued and criminal complaints were issued; the media was in overdrive reporting this slander.

Their attacks came so fast and furious it was literally head spinning. It became almost impossible to tune it out as they unleased one charge after another. Decent people were stalked, hounded and destroyed. To any observer it was impossible not to step away and look with disdain and disgust at the stories unfolding around them. If you held any position near President Trump there was a good chance you would be charged with something criminal or scandalous.

Constant rumors were floated about Trump's imminent removal from office. More 'fake' stories from unnamed sources came to light every day. 'Fake News; became a common word although prior to 2015 Americans had never heard of that term. It quickly became a part of everyday discussions in America. Unless you were a really good sleuth, it was nearly impossible to find the truth.

The obvious intention was to turn the tide of the Trump support against him. They intended to force his supporters to discard their 'frivolous and stupid' idea of supporting an outsider and return to their own idea of sanity. It would be forceful if they were not open to less than gentle persuasion.

Respected Generals, leaders and a host of others emerged from what we now know as 'The Swamp.' This was an 'elite' group of people who existed behind the scenes in our political arenas for so long many had become swamp creatures. 'Drain the Swamp' became the rallying cry across America. We had first heard the term when Donald Trump was campaigning for office. Suddenly we came face to face with the evil, vile and hate filled real swamp. It was sobering even while repulsive. Who could have guessed how dirty the swamp was?

Prior to that time, the generals had been more respected than the former leaders and other politicians. We believed in them; many now joined the ranks of exposed people at the top of our Intelligence Agencies and Security Apparatus's of the USA. It appeared that very few at the top of these agencies, including the Department of Defense, were acting honorably. We soon learned to trust the people under the top ranks, those who were out in the field. They had been well aware that their leaders had become corrupt but were helpless to change or expose it, until now.

Absolute power really does corrupt absolutely. We all witnessed it.

Another grave miscalculation was occurring as these events and new information emerged. The chaos and events that were intended to destroy the support of Donald Trump back-fired.

America is a nation that embraces justice; perhaps more than any nation in the world. We abhor injustice and revolt against it. While supporters were leery of the word 'witch-hunt' initially, we learned that it was accurate as time passed.

The winds of a righteous anger began to blow. This was wrong; no one in America wanted these kinds of actions to become a new normal in our public discourse. Equal treatment is in the DNA of the American people.

Donald Trump and his supporters were being treated to anything but that.

It was unacceptable to most Americans who did not have a political stake in the outcome. It was unforgivable to his supporters. It was a time to come together, and they did. Their ranks grew, silently, lest they become targets of violence and rage that had been unleashed against them.

10 THE PARADE OF THE SHAMS

Trump supporters were understandably stunned and angry at the manner they had been portrayed publicly. They were also disgusted with the disrespect they and President Trump were treated to, including that from the media and newspapers.

It was clear that the tactics of stalking and confronting people merely because of their political beliefs was unlawful; yet it occurred with regularity. America quickly began to feel like a country many no longer recognized. As they suffered these terrible indignities from total strangers, something far more sinister began to emerge.

The man they had supported was being publicly portrayed as an agent for Russia! 'Russia 'Russia Russia,' the words became a mantra with a new outrageous story emerging daily. The American people had never before witnessed this kind of an attack on their leader.

Day after day new allegations from 'unnamed sources' emerged in the press.

Their stories were further boosted by the media outlets as Americans were treated to non-stop coverage. Oddly enough, very few, if any, of the Trump supporters believed this was true. They had already been personally attacked and labeled as white supremacists, racists and the entire range of 'ists' ism's, and phobias that had become a part of the Democrat Party's dialogue about Trump supporters.

The unfair accusations hurled against them made it easy to believe that something was amiss with these new allegations. We quickly learned that 'unnamed sources' typically meant a story planted by someone with an agenda and rarely contained any facts. And so, we waited patiently for the proof.

The constant drumbeat of unverified allegations hurled at President Trump was soon combined with regular occurrences of mistreatment of his supporters. They were all paying close attention, waiting for proof of any of these preposterous allegations.

Once again, former FBI director James Comey took front and center stage. He appeared to confirm that he no evidence in his Senate hearings, yet he freely admitted to having leaked documents to a professor/friend to instigate the appointment of a special counsel to investigate Trump.

His statements sounded intentionally vague. To most who watched Comey's testimony he appeared angry and arrogant. In other words, he was quite full of himself and seemingly believed his actions could not be questioned. He spoke as though he and his actions were above the same laws we were all expected to obey.

Comey's testimony assured all of the supporters that President Trump had made the right choice to let the FBI Director go. He marched to the beat of a different drum; one most did not recognize nor had any interest in hearing.

The facts about the Russian collusion are on record. There never was any collusion, there was never any evidence of one and none of the investigators believed there had been. This is all a matter of record now.

A Special Council was appointed; two years and more than $30 million dollars was spent to learn what all of the investigators already knew. The allegations had no substance; there were no facts to support it. All the while media outlet anchors daily provided a new dose of 'facts' from an unnamed source. They assumed the duty of stoking a fire and did so diligently. The 'Impeachment' mantra was repeated daily. Pundits and those parading as experts gave their opinion about an imminent impeachment of our President.

Contents of our President's phone calls with foreign leaders were leaked. It was a dangerous practice to engage in. It was dangerous for our national security. Other nation's leaders no longer believed they could talk privately with the leader of the free world. This began to erode the trust of the people who had once believed our nation's leaders were honest. We were forced to look at and question the motives behind the people we had once believed in. This included the highest levels of our intelligence and security branches.

In their zeal to paint Trump as uniformed, ignorant and corrupt, they forced all of us to look long and hard at who was making the allegations and what was really behind their actions. It was necessary for us to consider the source before we could determine whether we could believe in that source. Unnamed sources no longer had any credibility in America.

What were not on record were the emotions of the people who supported President Trump. The press and the media had made a fatal error as they presented this barrage of misinformation to the public. They combined their illegitimate attacks on the president with their attacks on his supporters. We all became guilty of a crime that had never occurred. Not by our President and not by his supporters. This is what happens when unchecked zealots take control of any issue.

Reputations of highly respectful people were irreversibly besmirched. Those who were a part of the Trump Administration or his campaign came under unbearable scrutiny. Investigations, criminal charges and lawsuits were initiated randomly. Most had little or no merit but garnered hours of media coverage, all intended to slander and besmirch Donald Trump and anyone associated with him.

This was an all-out assault on a duly elected sitting president. Never before had the United States of America witnessed an attempted coup, until the election of Donald Trump.

These shenanigans were alarming to watch. They were a strong reminder of why our constitution was so important. Without it the American people would have experienced a third world coup.

The murmurs about a corrupt Ukraine call between President Trump and the new leader began just before the Mueller Investigation formerly concluded. Another coup attempt was in the making.

It's worth noting that throughout all of the time that was passing, the public was served heavy doses of 'unnamed sources' new information about all of the criminals and corruption around Donald Trump. Outlandish books were written, touted as having facts. It was a steady drumbeat that never ceased. It was also untrue. The media and Democrat Party had become spin masters of criminal intent.

It was an overload and many turned off the news. No one believed most of what they heard anymore. This was really tragic for the country. Our Intelligence Agencies and Security Apparatus of our nation had been exposed as having clay feet. We now knew beyond any doubt that the media was equally corrupt. Added to those sobering revelations was the recognition that the actors and actresses we had supported and held dear for years in Hollywood actually thought millions of Americans were stupid and useless. Their fame and wealth had been gained primarily through the efforts of the very people they regarded with utter disrespect and disdain.

Why? It was a good question; why were all these people from so many different factions creating such frenzy to cover up and make up outlandish stories? Why were they persecuting our president? Most supporters and many who had not supported the president began to take notice.

What was going on, and why? It was becoming more and more obvious that something was lurking beneath all of this. There was too much effort being expended to create a false narrative. Most Americans suspected something was amiss in a big way. And it was.

About the same time we watched Robert Mueller publically state that his panel of very biased attorneys had found no evidence of collusion, we began to learn of Nancy Pelosi's, (the Speaker of the House of Representatives) intent to impeach President Trump for the contents of a telephone call with the leader of Ukraine.

There was hardly a break before the Democrats were off to the next effort to remove President Trump from office.

Thus began a month's long journey to nowhere, again. The American people were treated to a new round of media blitzes with Representative Adam Schiff, Jerry Nadler, Chuck Schumer and Nancy Pelosi controlling the storyline that was trolled daily on the media outlets.

It was difficult to watch, particularly knowing the public had been given an opportunity to read the contents of the call. It had been recorded by several people as it happened. Nothing about the congratulatory call seemed extraordinary.

When President Trump mentioned Joe Biden's son in the call it was clearly an effort to learn the truth about some issues that were, and still are, deeply troubling to everyone who knows the story. Joe Biden was not a contender for any public office at that time. President Trump had a duty to ask about and learn the truth to protect the American people.

During the course of the impeachment trial we had been treated to multiple trips out to talk to the news media by Adam Schiff, Jerry Nadler and Nancy Pelosi to leak their version of what we had all heard. There appeared to be no end to the false scenarios being tossed about by the news media.

On and on the 'trial' went; more smears and slander were spread by these almost comic players in a real tragedy in America. There was no case for impeachment but the Democrats held the majority in the House and so they voted to impeach our President.

The case proceeded to the Senate where a final determination would be made. Two more weeks of trials passed. This time it was Senator Chuck Schumer who led the effort.

The entire nation received a great civic lesson as these proceedings were all televised. For students across America it was perhaps their first opportunity to learn how our government works. Civics had long since been removed from the school curriculum.

Finally, there was a vote; Donald Trump was found not guilty of the charges in the Senate .It was a 100% partisan vote. No Democrats voted to find him not guilty. This was no surprise to anyone. The Republicans held the majority in the Senate. There was no evidence to support the charges. Donald Trump was not, nor had he ever been, guilty of the charges.

Yet another episode was recorded in the shame of American politics. The Trump supporters grew increasingly weary of the ongoing attacks and complete lack of respect for the President of the United States.

Many who had never been a supporter of President Trump were appalled by what was transpiring in the nation's capital. The Democrats had set into motion the equivalent a 'fire' call in the theatre. They had unashamedly lied and misrepresented issues; they demanded prosecutions. Each time a great deal of tax payer dollars and time were expended only to learn the charges and accusations were false. Worse, the perpetrators had known they were false before they began.

The credibility of Congress was quickly eroding. The only thing polling lower than Congress was the media. The media had hit an all-time low. In a very silent manner, the American people were stating their own case.

Meanwhile, fact began to dribble out into public discourse about many of these people who had engaged in the continuing effort to remove President Trump. They were now becoming persons of great interest in investigations as the real facts began to emerge. This may provide a glimpse into why they were so doggedly determined to remove the President. None doubted that he would force the exposure of the facts as they became available. The curtain that covered their actions was about to be ripped away.

Most believed that crimes were being uncovered; the piper was on the way to collect. Big heads were likely to roll. That was likely the best explanation for the events that had been unfolding for the previous nearly 4 years.

Other things had been going on in the country while these political theatrics were on display, important things.

11 A NEW HORIZON AS THE ENGINE ROARS

'In just three short years, we have shattered the mentality of American decline, and we have rejected the downsizing of America's destiny.' ~President Donald J. Trump

Donald Trump understood the economy, possibly better than any president who preceded him. This was his arena and few could perform better. He led an economic resurgence that surpassed every record in history by the end of 2019. Wages were up significantly, finally. To date, 8 million new jobs and more than 500,000 manufacturing jobs have been added. The economy exceeded every CBO projection of three year job growth in 2019 alone. The unemployment level reached the lowest level in history for Black, Hispanic and Asian Americans. For women in the workforce, unemployment reached a 65 year low.

President Trump applied his belief of 'a rising tide lifts all boats' to every aspect of his presidency. His intention was clearly stated; he planned to lift up all Americans. More than 2.3 million prime age jobs were filled by 2019, up from 1.3 million in the previous administration.

The poverty rates for African Americans and Hispanic Americans hit new lows in 2018, long before the record breaking aspects of 2019.

Employment rates for African Americans, Hispanic Americans, Asian Americans, including those without a high school degree; even disabled Americans had reached record highs. Six million Americans were lifted out of poverty, including 1.4 million children. The poverty rates for African Americans and Hispanic Americans hit new lows. Donald Trump was successful in lifting all people to a place where the American Dream could be realized.

President Trump initiated and signed historic tax reform, ensuring that the lowest wage earners would enjoy faster wage gains than any other income group. The net wealth of the bottom half of American households grew by almost 50 percent, more than three times the rate of growth for the upper half.

The President's historic cuts to regulation increased American household incomes by $6,500 a year. The energy revolution saved every household $2500 a year in heating and electricity costs.

With rapid speed our President began ridding the country of regulations that were crippling and killing the US economy and individual income opportunity. Every new regulation required at last two old ones to be removed. In truth, there were far more than 2 for each new one. On many occasions 26 or more old regulations were replaced by one new one.

The handcuffs came off of businesses. They were encouraged to thrive and grow, both large and small; entrepreneurs breathed a sigh of relief. They expressed their belief that businesses had been under attack for 8 years; finally they could grow their businesses.

We watched as President Trump traveled to the G7 meetings for the first time. He insisted that members of NATO finally begin to pay their fair share of billions of dollars in delinquent payments. American taxpayers had been paying the bill for the defense of wealthy nations for years. No doubt it made many foreign leaders uncomfortable but it was the right action to take; it worked. He was looking out for Americans; it was a new day for the taxpayers.

Donald Trump renegotiated one major contract after another. Americans began to understand the benefit of having a leader who understood the economy, not only of America, but also of foreign nations. He understood from his own business abroad what those nations needed and how to negotiate and meet in the middle.

For the US this translated to a new kind of winning. Years of inept negotiations had taken a terrible toll on our economy and job losses. There really is an art to making not just any deal, but rather, a good and fair deal.

Reprisal tariffs were placed on nations that had spent 40 years taking advantage of America. Trump refused to play on any field until it was leveled for America. This was shocking to all; never before had an American leader demanded an equal playing field. We learned that our former and current leaders in Congress had no appetite for a level playing field. We saw fear in their eyes. But the tide had begun to turn.

The North America Fair Trade Agreement, (NAFTA) a job killing trade alliance passed under President Clinton, was replaced. President Trump negotiated with Mexico and Canada and reached an agreement to replace it with the United States–Mexico–Canada Agreement (USMCA). All three countries ratified it by March 2020. This created an enormous boost to manufacturing, farm and trade opportunities in the United States.

President Trump withdrew the US from the Trans Pacific Trade Agreement (TPP) which would have killed our auto industry. Hundreds of thousands of jobs were saved.

Equally, if not more important, President Trump dared to go where no other president had gone before. He confronted China and stared them straight in the eye over years of rampant theft of American jobs, intellectual properties and trade deficits. He refused to be bullied or settle for less than what was fair to the American People.

The results of Phase 1 of the China Trade Agreement, something that seemed impossible before the Trump effect, was incredible wealth returning to America. Tariffs were imposed on goods being shipped to the USA.

Intellectual properties and trade rights were enforced with severe economic penalties imposed if they were violated. An agreement to purchase goods, especially farm crops returned wealth back to American farmers who had been targeted by China as they tried to punish Trump and turn his supporters against them. The agreement collected $50 billion in tariffs. $28 billion was returned directly back to the farmers from the tariffs to repay the damage they had caused in their boycott.

Manipulation of the Chinese currency was forbidden, along with giving the

USA access to Chinese finance services for US companies. Trump has announced plans to work with the World Trade Organization to negotiate fair trade deals. Currently China is treated as a developing nation, providing opportunities and benefits not available to the US. He has promised to tackle that issue in his second term; another playing field that needs to be leveled.

While the playing field was not yet leveled with China, that was to come in Phase 2. But there was a new trade landscape in America; everyone benefitted.

12 MIGHTY MIGHT

The military might of America was legendary, having gained a stellar reputation by the end of World War 2. It was, without question, the most respected military in the world.

During the Obama Administration the US military began draw downs on nuclear weapons and entered a sequestration where funding for military dwindled dramatically.

The troops were given new rules for engagement in war; morale dropped dramatically, as did the level of equipment and maintenance in military vehicles. By the end of that administration our military was probably in the weakest position it had been in since the beginning of World War 2.

Ammunition was in short supply, our ships and planes mostly belonged in the graveyard where mechanics had been forced to look for parts to attempt to repair the existing ones.

The men and women in our military felt denigrated by the treatment they received from the administration and the fall out effects of that overseas.

We watched in horror as Iran captured a US ship and forced our sailors to kneel with their hands behind their backs. This was a new page in history for America. We were kneeling before a military they could have destroyed on command. This was not lost on any American. It was unthinkable and unacceptable.

NASA, the pride of our space program had been shut down. Grass was growing on the runways. The American space program was forced to 'hitch' rides with the Russian Cosmonauts. A slow burning rage was growing in many. American exceptionalism was scoffed at and apologized for. Morale was low in the nation. By almost any perception, it appeared that America was in decline.

During the 2016 presidential campaign we heard a lot about the Iran Nuclear Deal that Donald Trump was certain was bad for America. It offered little, if any, protection to the US and endangered Israel. It was that transaction under which the former administration delivered, under the cover of darkness, $1.5 billion dollars, $1.2 billion in cash to Iran. This angered many Americans and outraged the Republicans in Congress. Iranians were in the streets daily shouting, 'Death to Americans' and burning our flag. Even worse, they were the number one sponsor of terrorism in the world.

At a time when Al Qaeda, the Taliban and ISIS were causing havoc across the globe, the money was sent to Iran who distributed it to their Revolutionary Army and funded those same groups.

Our closest ally in the Middle East, Israel, and many other nations felt betrayed by these actions.

The Trump Administration immediately began the task of rebuilding our military. In short order more than $2 Trillion dollars was invested in new planes, ships, submarines and equipment, all made in the USA. The military reassumed the position of the most powerful in the world within three years under his administration.

Technology had been advancing across the globe. Donald Trump recognized early in his presidency that space was where far too much action was occurring that could be very dangerous to the USA. In response to that he added the sixth branch of our military, The Space Force. Not since the Air Force was formed 75 years before had America added a new branch of the Armed Services. It was both exciting and necessary.

Both Democrats and the mainstream Republicans, who came to be known as RHINOS, warned us that Donald Trump was a war monger who would quickly get the US into foreign wars. Very early in his administration we had good cause to pause as we were introduced to the MOAB bomb, nicknamed the mother of all bombs We learned over time that Donald Trump was, as he had told us, a peacemaker, but one who used strength to make peace.

The ISIS Caliphate, Al Qaeda and the Taliban were systematically defeated. Land that had been forcefully taken was returned to its rightful owner. Our military who had been engaged in wars for more than 19 years began to win, and return home.

Perhaps an unintended consequence of the actions the Obama Administration had taken by delivering so much cash to Iran was the utter fear it instilled in other countries in the Middle East. They would be quickly outgunned and were left with little if any way to defend their countries. As they took a fresh look at the landscape around them, most determined that Israel posed the least threat and had the most capability to help them defend their nations.

Donald Trump had been working on a Middle East peace agreement almost since the time he had taken office. Many before him had tried but always their efforts delivered no lasting results. It seemed an impossible task. His son-in-law, Jared Kushner, was Jewish and had a deep interest in working towards peace for the Middle East. He joined an entourage of people appointed by Donald Trump and worked diligently for three years to craft an acceptable agreement. A part of that was recognizing Jerusalem as the Capital of Israel. This had been promised by almost every American president while they were campaigning but had never materialized.

In September 2020 The White House held a ceremony for the signing of the Middle East Peace Accord between Israel, the UAE and Bahrain. Nine other nations are currently in talks to join the accord. This was considered historic and biblical. It was made possible because of Trump's insistence of talking to those we considered to be enemies and the efforts of attempting to find common ground.

President Trump told us he had been warned by President Obama as he was leaving office that North Korea was armed with Nuclear weapons and posed the most pressing foreign threat. We were near war.

He employed the same strategy with the North Korean leader. He sent Secretary of State Mike Pompeo to North Korea to talk to the leader of the Hermit Kingdom. By June 30, 2019 President Trump had accompanied Kim Jung Un across the dematerialized zone and shook hands. He was determined to try to forge peace where possible, while ensuring that every nation became aware of the value of trading with and becoming an ally of the USA.

President Trump established trust with these nations by being trustworthy. It paid off in a big way when they joined together to find common ground and re-establish normal relations.

In 2020 he was nominated for three Nobel Peace Prizes; a first ever for an American President. Not a single network news station reported this achievement initially, but the supporters and most of the world looked on in awe of the accomplishments of Donald Trump.

13 PROMISES MADE PROMISES KEPT

As the next election approached Americans began seeing signs around the famous Trump rallies stating, 'Promises Made Promises Kept.' This was new for us as promises were not something any politician wants to talk about at reelection time. They almost never keep any of theirs; Trump had kept all of them and exceeded his promises.

He had promised to appoint Conservative Judges to the Supreme Court; he appointed three. He also filled more than 200 Federal Judgeships with Conservative, principled judges who are likely to deliver findings consistent with our constitutional rights.

He promised to build a wall on our Southern border. More than 400 miles have been completed with a 30 foot wall that rivals the imagination. This was not an easy accomplishment as Congress fought him at every turn, took him to court when he reallocated funds and finally ended the battle in the Supreme Court. Our Southern border is probably safer today than it has been in history. He promised that Mexico would pay for the wall; they are collecting at the border crossing to complete the wall. More than 27,000

Mexican soldiers have guarded the border while the wall is being built. More than 500,00 alien criminals have been deported.

He promised to find solutions that would effectively deal with the opioid crisis. He formed the Presidents Commission on Combating Drug Addiction and the Opioid Crisis. An alliance was forged with Columbia and Mexico to stop the distribution and trafficking in drugs. By 2019 the US experienced the first decline in drug use in many years. Rehabilitation centers to assist users in recovering were opened.

He promised to rebuild the military and did so. Today it is without any competition the strongest in the world.

He promised to renegotiate trade deals; the worst have been renegotiated favorably for every American.

He promised to return manufacturing jobs to the US. More than 700,000 have now been returned. Many new factories are under construction that will create even more good paying jobs.

He promised to negotiate deals for peace and bring our military home from endless foreign wars; that has been accomplished.

He promised an economic recovery that was vital to the US. The stock market has broken records more than 70 times under his guidance. The American economic recovery has been the envy of the world.

He promised to defeat ISIS and negotiate peace on the Korean border. ISIS was obliterated; its leader hunted down and killed. The leading terrorist in the world, Iran's General Qasem Soleimani, was killed. North Korea has agreed to a total denuclearization of the Korean peninsula.

He promised to deal with religious persecution. He signed an Executive Order promoting Free Speech and Religious Liberty. An ambassador for our religious freedom was appointed to introduce it into our foreign affairs. Donald Trump had been more vocal and acted more strongly for religious rights than any leader before him.

He promised tax reform and delivered the biggest tax cut for the American people and businesses in history. This returns almost $10,000 in cash and benefits annually to Americans.

He promised a pro-life agenda and has taken extensive steps to dismantle Title X of the Public Health and Human Service Act to prevent further funding where abortion is encouraged as family planning. He discontinued the funding of United Nations Population Fund (UNFPA) in support of his administration's anti-abortion policies. He also pushed to unite Congress around the preservation of life through the defunding of Planned Parenthood.

He promised to be pro-Israel. He formerly recognized Jerusalem as the undivided capital of Israel. He re-located the US Embassy from Tel Aviv to Jerusalem fulfilling one more promise. Benjamin Netanyahu stated that he considers President to be the best friend Israel has ever had.

President Trump promised to address the minority disparities in housing and income. He has lifted 6 million people out of poverty and created more jobs than any president in history that benefitted minority groups. He established opportunity zones to assist in building businesses in the low income communities to help them rebuild their communities.

He promised to address the educational disparities in America for low income households. Across America school choice has been offered and accepted, ensuring that every child gets the chance they deserve. He is promising to make this available to every child during his second term if elected.

He promised to fix the mistreatment of our Veterans who were mistreated for years at VA hospitals. Trump has honored his promisd to deal with that. He was able to get VA Choice and VA Accountability approved.

He went after Big Pharm to address the overcharging on all of America's pharmaceuticals. Americans were paying the highest prices in the world, subsidizing other nations. He negotiated for a 'Favored Nation's Status' ensuring that the US would pay the lowest prices available in the world as they were the largest consumer. Those price cuts take effect on January 1, 2021.

He promised to try to correct the time that was required to get approval for new drugs. Many Americans had terminal diseases and were forced to travel abroad for medicines and treatments. Those who did not have the funds to travel were left to die. Trump negotiated with the drug companies and the federal government to secure a 'Right to Try' the new drugs that were promising. This action saved many lives in our nation.

The 'Promises Made Promises Kept' mantra is a byproduct of a rising tide lifts all boats. When you attempt to make life better for everyone, we all rise above the waterline.

Donald Trump promised to bring patriotism back to America, to make every American proud again. He sought to erase the decline of the past 16 years. He realized the lean to Socialism had begun in the schools. He initiated Patriotic Education back into education. His administration also identified and cut funding for programs that were teaching our children anti American ideas.

The Trump supporters and President have much to be proud of, and they are. He gathers tremendous crowds at every rally because he cares about the people and loves America. It shows in every action he takes.

Every time Donald Trump wins another battle or takes another day to fly out and speak to the American people, meets the press and answers all of their questions (no matter how outrageous they may be) or dares to remind us that we are one nation under God his supporters grow in number. Their bet seems safer than ever to them.

14 CHINA'S CALLING CARD

By the end of 2019 the American economy was they envy of every nation in the world. We had long since left any fear of China's dominance in the dust behind us. We were preparing to engage in Phase 2 of the China Trade Agreement. The US was energy independent and now an energy exporter around the globe. Every conceivable economic and jobs record had been broken by the Trump Administration. He was the undisputed champion of the leaders.

This did not endear Trump to many other leaders, in fact quite the opposite. Very wealthy people had been betting on China for a long time and had no desire to see them pay tariffs or to be held accountable. They were betting against the American middle class who bore the burden of those terrible negotiations. Many of these are the same people who talk about compassion and caring and all the liberal talking points. If they were ever sincere it does not show in their actions. The middle class had been treated like plow horses until the Trump Administration took command.

The meeting for the China Davos deal began on January 21, 2020. China was easily the biggest loser in the new negotiations. They had spent decades stealing from the American economy. They were not happy to be entering this 2nd phase with the Trump Administration. The US was by then considered the hottest economy in the world.

From that vantage point there was no reasonable argument not to easily re-elect Donald Trump.

By late January 2020 our news began to show images of terrible things occurring in Wuhan, China. It was presented as a deadly virus that was wreaking havoc in that province. There were horrifying videos of people screaming and crying in hospital hallways, and others being forcefully dragged from their homes. We were thankful that China was a long way from us. But it not long enough.

In his State of the Union address the President mentioned the terrible time China was having with a virus that was likely to become an epidemic. On January 31, 2020, less than 2 weeks after the negotiations for Phase 2 with China had taken place, President Trump placed a ban on entry from China to the US. He was mostly ridiculed for that action both by the media and his advisors. The US had one confirmed death by that time from a disease that became known as Covid-19.

Shortly afterwards a representative of the Center for Disease Control (CDC) was featured on news programs advising that we should all prepare for a significant interruption in our daily lives. We heard her, but had no idea what that meant or how it might affect any part of America.

Soon after, President Trump initiated a travel ban on Europe, with the exception of the UK and a scant few others. Something serious was going on; it was obvious to everyone by then. The economy Trump was so proud of was going to be interrupted in a very big way with these travel bans. Those who had been paying any attention to his efforts knew he would never llow it unless there was no other safe way.

China denied entry to any of our investigators to determine the origin of the virus or to offer assistance. They had earlier assured us it could not transmit to humans as it had originated from bats at a wet market. In the beginning, things were pretty baffling. The virus had not spread to other areas in China. Wuhan was on a strict lockdown with horror stories escaping from doctors and nurses. Many quickly disappeared, forever.

The World Health Organization (WHO) took the position that there was no need to panic; the virus was not expected to cause widespread interruption in other countries. They told us China was doing an excellent job of containing it. We would soon learn that China had a tremendous influence on the information spread through the WHO. The virus spread around the word, quickly reaching epidemic status.

We were seeing images of Chinese doctors wearing the equivalent of hazmat suits while treating patients. There was stark fear in the faces of the Chinese people. Soon there were images of makeshift hospitals and tales of 8000 bodies waiting at morgues. Many scorned China's lack of medical care, never dreaming they would soon see those images in their own cities. America continued on with day to day life.

By early March we began seeing images from Europe, particularly Italy. Bodies were being stored for disposal; caskets were lined up in open areas waiting to be claimed and then, the unimaginable. Entire countries were locked down. We saw images of Paris, Rome and London with animals running down the streets. There were no people, no cars, no sign of life.

You Tube was filled with videos from people attempting to survive the changes. We wept and mourned with them as we learned that a cut off age was established to determine who they would try to save. People were dying by the tens of thousands.

On March 16 President Donald Trump held a press conference surrounded by Vice President Mike Pence, Dr. Anthony Fauci, Dr. Deborah Birx and the leader of the CDC. They announced a plan for 15 days to slow the spread of Covid-19. Each states Governor was charged with the responsibility of making a determination about who was an essential worker or business and the rules their state must adhere to. The USA was shutting down with the exception of essential workers. The time would be spent developing new testing, locating Personal Protection for the medical workers and retooling plants to make ventilators. The goal was to prevent US hospitals, ICU units and ER's from being overwhelmed. No elective surgeries were permitted. Schools, places of businesses, factories, restaurants and bars all closed. Our economy almost ground to a halt.

The President formed a task force to respond daily to the people. He held a lengthy press conference daily to update the nation. He was surrounded by members of the task force, doctors, distributors and a host of businesses who had voluntarily joined the efforts. Donald Trump joined the private sector with our government resources and when necessary invoked the Wars Act to force factories to make PPE and ventilators. Private labs from across the nation joined the fight. Researchers went into high gear to develop a vaccine. The virus had reached pandemic status; 188 nations were afflicted with it. The global death toll would surpass a million by the time of this writing.

The President developed 'Project Warp Speed' for the researchers and the FDA to eliminate unnecessary red tape and get therapeutics and vaccines to the people as quickly as possible. An untold number of lives would eventually be saved by this action. The time to get the new advances to the people was moved forward by as much as two years.

It is a good time to stop and imagine how President Trump, who had performed beyond anyone's greatest expectations on his promises and was leading a nation that had become the envy of the world, must have felt.

Through no fault of his own or anyone he had any measure of control over, everything he had worked so hard for came crashing down very quickly. The weight of the world now lay, literally, on his shoulders. Every nation was rapidly losing lives. They had nowhere near enough protection for the health care workers or those who responded to the emergencies. Tele-Health was born and will probably continue on in America.

China selectively delivered orders for the PPE and vital medicines. Somehow in that NAFTA deal China had pretty much taken control of the US drug manufacturing market. Suddenly they were refusing to ship medicines. It became a bidding war with the highest bidder getting the now coveted PPE and medicines.

Each day another emergency arose. New York began to resemble Italy with bodies waiting in refrigerated trucks to be claimed outside of hospitals and funeral homes. Finally, NY was forced to create mass burials where the caskets were piled on top of each other and then covered. Thousands of people were dying daily in the US and across the globe.

Americans were covered with face masks when they could find them; the 15 days to slow the spread became 30 and then reverted to whatever date each Governor determined was safe to re-open. Three stages were offered by the CDC to reopen states. Many still remain under some kind of lockdown status more than 7 months later.

President Trump and the US Congress put together a Cares Act that would eventually cost American taxpayers more than $6 trillion dollars in an effort to maintain the businesses, subsidize and assist with unemployment in the states, provide free Covid testing and health care and stimulus checks to every American earning less than $150.000. They understood that in the midst of all the emergencies, the economy had to be stabilized, the people protected from all the other side effects of a lockdown. It was a monumental effort. Every American can be proud of the accomplishments made during this time.

While there was finger pointing and scathing comments from much of the media, a few, like Tucker Carlson at FOX News decided to behave like a journalist and go searching for the truth. He quickly located two labs in Wuhan China in close proximity to the outbreak. One was a lab that Anthony Fauci was reported to have made a large investment in, along with other US investors. Across and down the street was a government lab where bio weapons were developed for China. He showed pictures and maps making note of both of them.

Although US investigative teams were blocked from entering China, we soon learned that the virus had not originated in the wet markets of China; it had instead escaped from one of the two labs which are in the area. One has been boarded up now; it seems reasonable to assume that is the one where it originated.

Still, the virus that had spread to 188 countries had not spread through China. Some arrived at the conclusion that China had controlled the virus, preventing it from spreading to their country while being untruthful about it to the rest of the world.

Catastrophic damage was caused around the globe by Covid-19. We have yet to learn the total of the trillions of dollars that were lost to all of the nations. UK sued China in the World Court for $6 trillion in damages. Europe and many other nations are now in the midst of a second round of Covid -19 that is causing more lockdowns and tremendous losses.

The State of Emergency that has spread around the world has kept most of the attention focused on a treatment and a cure. Still, looking back, there were signs we all missed that something might be on the horizon. In October 2019 another meeting was held in NY by some of the same investors and billionaires we have come to learn much more about. They emerged with white pillows with a blue lettered word 'Covid -19' embossed on the front. This was long before China or anyone else had named the virus.

In 2017 Dr. Anthony Fauci released a statement that Donald Trump's presidency would encounter a pandemic. If none of us knew it was coming, it appears a select few did have some inkling that our future might not look the same as we were accustomed to.

The US has lost more than 210,000 Americans to this dreaded disease; it creeped into our lives like a thief who attacked in the night. We did not see or hear it coming yet it transformed all of our lives. We were denied the opportunity of even having a funeral and in some instances, or even a properly burial. Every system was tested, many were overcome.

To most Americans this has felt very much like a war that must be won at all costs; because it is. American ingenuity has taken front and center stage as our researchers and labs were forced to stretch to the limits of their vision to find an answer. We call them heroes today, along with many others. They have performed admirably, as have our front line workers in the health care system. Truckers who deliver the goods that are essential were finally recognized for their contribution. So too were the grocery workers, cashiers, and so many others who had before been taken for granted.

Americans may never have realized how restaurants and theatres had become a staple in their lives until it was no longer possible to visit them. We had never given a second thought to our children attending school, until they could not. Probably no one ever expected to see Times Square in NY empty, not a single car on the street cameras. Families gathered in their homes and found ways to keep some kind of normalcy in their lives. Wearing a mask became as common place as wearing a shirt when we went out.

Democrats and the left wing media shifted into high gear to demonize our President while newscasters around the world marveled at his accomplishments. In a time when our country needed to pull together the same efforts to divide us were amped up. This was one of the more shameful things that happened during the pandemic.

Perhaps the very most shameful thing was Nancy Pelosi's complete unwillingness to work towards an acceptable agreement with Congress to find an acceptable agreement that would provide a stimulus check to Americans that were hurting terribly. The plight of the people meant nothing to her; there was an election looming. She had no intention of allowing a stimulus check to boost the Trump economy. The hatred that all of the previous efforts had stoked took control of some of our leaders. They lost their way so completely they seemed to have forgotten that they were sent to Washington to represent their own constituents.

Meanwhile, across America the people were doing everything in their power to piece their lives back together, to hold their families together. Many became closer; some fell apart. It was a tragedy of epic proportions. We were given the opportunity to see the best and the worst of the people we had elected. Where the contrived hatred did not exist, there was great pride in the leadership of Donald Trump, Mike Pence and all of the people who worked diligently on the task force.

China's calling card of Covid-19 may well have been yet another attempt to fell the American President and his incredible achievements in the economy. It did not work; the economy is roaring back; the people who supported him before had a whole new reverence for his ability. They knew now, more than ever, that he would do everything possible to help them recover and continue their own American dream. Score one more for the President.

15 FROM CHAOS TO CLARITY

The recovery from Covid-19 proved to be a long winding road. America re-opened in phases. It was difficult at times to know which state offered what services to the people. Things had changed in a big way. In many ways it was a somber spring and summer in the US. There was great pain and loss, a normal level of anger that was to be expected and a time of hope and small celebrations as things slowly began to reopen.

Governors across the country rose or fell into a heap of rubble by their decisions on maintaining safety and re-opening. Adding to the mix was the upcoming election.

America was wounded, but the eagle would certainly still soar. The Trump supporters never doubted it. The left wing liberals and media were infuriated because his supporter's faith was not broken. While they exaggerated every perceived slight and spewed out more hatred, the Trump supporters got into their boats and cars where they were safely distanced and formed their own rallies on the water and in the streets. Trump 2020 flags were everywhere in the country. They had not silenced his supporters;

they had inspired that same old Yankee ingenuity that had made America great many times before. We were not surprised when the Democrats opened the next chapter in their Saul Alinsky evil playbook.

When George Floyd encountered the officers in Minneapolis the perfect opportunity presented itself. There were justifiable protests for abhorrent behavior of the officers that led to his death on the street. There was probably no one in America who did not support peaceful protests. We had witnessed a horrific scene that should never have happened in America. Again, righteous anger was on full display in America.

It began with people blocking the streets and challenging the drivers and quickly became violent. For them, it was time to take to the streets, with riots, looting and burning our cities.

What happened after those protests began introduced a whole new world of violence in America. Groups that were actually gangs, like Antifa and Black Lives Matter, arrived by bus and plane. They overtook the peaceful protests and turned them into riots.

Minneapolis was the first of these cities, many more followed. Entire blocks were burned down. Businesses owned by both black and white Americans were destroyed, stores were looted and people lost their lives. It was violent vengeance for a cause that was kept well under the radar.

These people who had been bussed in and had flown in to create this kind of chaos and violence were paid anarchists, intent on the total destruction of the foundation of America. It would become so ugly and vile we could hardly imagine it was happening in America.

Seattle Washington gave up six blocks to a group called 'CHAZ' that soon transitioned into 'CHOP.' From that encampment rose the movement to defund the police. They reduced 'CHOP' to three blocks that included the police precinct they had originally overtaken. There were fires, threats and seemingly a new city within a city had been born. A far left Mayor combined with a Democrat Governor allowed this to continue for weeks.

A nineteen year old boy who was just curious visited the scene in his city. He was shot dead in the streets. Shortly afterwards another person was shot. The police and first responders were not permitted in to help. Finally, President Trump advised the Mayor that our National Guard and Military Police were coming in one day later. She immediately ordered the area cleared and returned the streets back to the people. What she had once called a 'Love Fest, Summer of Love' had become a murder scene. $500 million dollars of damage was left in their wake.

Portland Oregon followed suit. Violent riots, looting and burnings of businesses were a nightly occurrence. There was an attempt to take over the Federal Building in the city. Federal Officers were blinded, many permanently, by commercial lasers. Gunshots and fire bombs became their normal for more than 100 days.

Chicago, New York, LA and finally Atlanta burst into flames with riots, looting, burning buildings and gunshots. Children were shot and killed in their Grandmothers back yards and on their own front porches. They were killed in their beds as they slept, in strollers and while walking down their own streets.

Lafayette Park across from the White House was overtaken. Mobs began tearing down National Monuments. The 'Church of the Presidents' was set on fire; nothing was sacred. Pure evil was unleashed on America. It was both frightening and reprehensible.

Democrats and the left wing media called these peaceful protests while blocks of cities burned in the background of their broadcasts. Little mention was made of the children and adults who had died or lost their businesses. They rallied the cry to defund the police, insisting law enforcement was the cause of all of the violence. Portland, Seattle, NY and LA all reduced funding for their police departments. All law enforcement was demonized nightly.

Streets across America were filled with protesters. Cities that had just reopened were now jam packed with strangers, packed together shouting, looting and rioting. The left wing liberals found no issues with these massive volumes of people in the streets, most not wearing a mask and all certainly not socially distanced.

Statutes were being torn down across our nation. National Monuments were defaced. There were threats to establish new police free areas like the 'CHOP" zones. America's history was being erased, violently.

President Trump reinstated a very old statue that made it a mandatory sentence of ten years in prison for anyone who tore down a statute or monument on Federal property. Only one instance in Portland has occurred where two statutes were torn down since.

To most observers it began to appear that the violence, rioting and looting was all part of a grand plan to frighten the Trump supporters into not voting for him in the upcoming election. For those who faithfully watched, the liberal left wind media called the riots 'peaceful protests.' When there was no way to avoid talking about the damages and murders, they portrayed it as a result of the angry white supremacist Trump supporters.

As the election approached we witnessed Joe Biden, the Democrat candidate, sequestered in his basement wearing a mask and reading haphazardly from a teleprompter. He appeared dazed and confused.

There was a great effort by the media outlets to cover his obvious inability to hold coherent thoughts together or the persistent stopping in the middle of a sentence because he could not find his way back to the sentence he was trying to form. Even his supporters did not, and still do not, expect him to serve a full term if elected. He was struggling mightily. Those who were not caught up in demonizing Donald Trump, the normal voter, openly voiced their concern about his health and his wife's willingness to allow him to continue.

In stark contrast Donald Trump planned an Independence Celebration at Mount Rushmore in South Dakota. It proved to be one of the best speeches of his presidency. The setting was beautiful. Millions of dollars of fireworks ended the evening. It was a proud and patriotic celebration.

We later learned the fireworks were negotiated in the Phase 1 China Trade Agreement; this beautiful night was curtesy of the Chinese government. It was all the sweeter knowing they had paid the bill.

16 LOUD AND PROUD

The RNC convention was held on the grounds of the White House; it was an incredibly patriotic and pro American event that would instill pride and patriotism in Americans. It was a well-planned and professional event that lasted four days. The event culminated with President Trump's acceptance of the nomination as the 2020 candidate for Presidency representing the RNC. Even with Covid-19 guidelines in place, the event will long be remembered a beacon of hope, a time to heal and restart the nation.

One week prior the DNC held their event to nominate Joe Biden as their candidate. It was mostly a virtual event, filled with negativity, fear mongering and hatred for Donald Trump. It was difficult to watch. I cannot imagine any participant enjoyed being a part of it. Negativity repels the human spirit.

Shortly after the RNC Convention wrapped up, the 2020 Trump campaign began in earnest. Mayors and Governors of many states had forbidden any rallies due to the Covid-19 restrictions. The Trump campaign planned events only to have the Democrat Governor's refuse to allow them to hold the rallies. In spite of the ongoing riots and protests in their streets, an event where masks and testing would be available was deemed too dangerous.

The Trump campaign renamed them to 'peaceful protests.' There was little the Governors and Mayors could say about a protest, as they continued to allow their streets to be filled with protesters and rioters.

There was a general air of resignation in the news media about the Trump Peaceful Protests. They realized that Trump could hold the protests but had little faith that very many people would show up. They seemed to feel very secure in the efforts that had been made to destroy him. And so, they waited to see him humiliated. Would anyone show up or still support him, they wondered?

The rallies after the reopening of America broke all of President Trump's previous records in attendance. They were held in Airport hangars, using the sunshine and fresh air to combat the ongoing Covid-19 issues. Tens of thousands of people waited to see Air Force 1 pull up to the protest (rally) sites. Their cheers were so loud they rivaled any NFL football game.

Events were scheduled several times a week. The rally attendance was massive. A celebratory atmosphere permeated the events with people arriving many hours prior to the starting time, hoping for a good location to see their President. There was dancing and music; a party like atmosphere surrounded every rally.

Soon there was no longer any doubt that all of the lies, the 'witch hunt,' the smears and terrible actions taken by people in authority positions, nor the impeachment and the Covid-19 crisis had not dimmed the enthusiasm of the supporters of Donald Trump. They showed up in droves.

At an exciting North Carolina rally the crowd suddenly broke into roaring chants of, "We Love YOU!" the noise was deafening. This open display of love for a President was the first time ever recorded in American history. These Americans sincerely loved their President.

President Trump took time off from his campaign rallies to announce Amy Coney Barrett as his 3rd Supreme Court Justice nominee. Rallies were scheduled throughout that week following the Rose Garden ceremony.

Just a few days later President Trump, the First Lady Melania Trump and their youngest son Barron tested positive for the dreaded virus. This was devastating news to the Trump supporters and much of the country. That same day we learned that Hope Hicks, the Communications Director for the administration had also tested positive. Soon thirty six people in total who had attended the Rose Garden ceremony had tested positive. Everyone was a Republican. It may be the first time that no Democrats had attended such an important event.

Donald Trump was transported to Walter Reed Medical Center one day after Americans learned he had tested positive. It was sobering to witness our President boarding Marine One to be transported to Walter Reed Medical Center with Covid -19.

Crowds gathered outside the facility in Bethesda, Maryland. The size grew and grew as supporters lined the streets, praying and holding candlelight vigils. Many never left. They camped out and waited. Public prayers were recited several times a day. The sidewalks were covered with people, those who had supported him and those who simply did not want to see their President in such a dangerous position. The American and Trump 2020 flags blew in the wind amid chants for the President.

The streets were clogged with cars blowing horns in support of the vigil, day and night.

His supporters said they had brought the rally to him when he could not come to them. Their devotion was obvious to all. Not until he was released three days later did the crowd clear the streets and sidewalks. Loud cheers were heard as Marine One lifted off and circled the crowd, returning the President to the White House.

What is the inspiration that drives people to support Donald Trump, and some to attend as many as 90+ rallies? Others who were not able to attend have never missed a single rally; they instead have watched on television. All of these people feel the need to participate in every event, to watch every Press Briefing he attends and to watch his interviews on television. Ask them why and they readily recite so many reasons.

They have watched for years as politicians came into office filled with promises they never intended to keep. Donald Trump had kept every promise.

He had been attacked unmercifully by the press, the media and Congress. Not a single thing he had been accused of had proved true. Instead they learned that his accusers had employed one of the directives from the Saul Alinsky book (a satanic book) and accused him of the very actions they had been engaged in. Americans found this repulsive.

Trump was a multi-billionaire. He did not need the job or the harassment directed at him. In fact, he worked for free, donating his $400,000+ salary to various charities.

No matter how outrageous his claims had been, each time he had been correct. He was brutally honest.

He was ruthless in the pursuit of rebuilding America back to her days of glory; he fully intended that every American could rise with the tide. He was tough when necessary and gentle when it was appropriate. Many felt he was a kind of father figure they trusted.

He had been unjustly accused of crimes he did not commit and brutalized at every turn, yet he continued on to the goals he had set. He was betrayed by many; those people were finally replaced by honest people with shared goals.

The American people came to understand that his motives were genuinely an effort to rebuild the nation and protect the citizens. He was qualified and capable; history may record him as more so than any predecessor. Americans soon learned that the people they had entrusted to lead their country had betrayed them at every turn. Corruption had taken hold in America and they were sickened by it.

Every unjust effort made by the liberal left wing, Congress and the media to harm him made them more determined to protect him.

Should anyone ask him how he planned to accomplish overturning that kind of corruption he would surely have answered that his army was God and the American people. They were on the same side; they were comprised of multitudes of people.

These people believe that Donald Trump is their last, best hope to pull their country back from the brink that leads to communism. Our military soldiers have said, 'He's the kind of man you would run through a brick wall for.' He inspires trust and loyalty. He is an anomaly because generations have passed since the American people have witnessed this kind of commitment, maybe never from a man who needed nothing at all from them.

In the midst of utter chaos and violence in our streets, and the terrible idea to defund the police, Donald Trump stood strong with law enforcement. Americans depended on him to maintain this position for their own safety.

He is witty, charismatic and as intelligent as any leader we have ever seen on the job. He is also a fighter who always intends to win. Donald Trump fights for and protects the American people, regardless of who they may be. He stands with our Constitution that protects all of us. It is for these reasons we love this President. Those who have paid attention without bias understand that loving our country is probably hise most important asset.

No longer in hiding, the Trump supporters are now loud and proud of him and of their support for Donald Trump. This is the Trump we love to LOVE.

ABOUT THE AUTHOR

Politics is not a subject I have ever addressed in a book, although I confess to have written many articles about people that probably cross over into politics around them. It is a fairly new ides in America that any person can be defined by their politics, probably not a healthy one.

Personally I have always been proud to have listened to the candidates and voted for the one I thought best represented what I hoped to see in America. Consequently, I have voted for both parties candidates. Something ugly has been creeping into the American political arena over the past few elections. Americans have been encouraged to turn against their fellow citizens; identity politics have taken a firm hold in the USA. I think this is growing more and more dangerous. The very rights we have all cherished, particularly our first and second amendments have been under steady attack. It has been shocking for me to see how easily our nation has been willing to pretend not to see what is happening or examine what that can mean in their lives.

When Donald Trump ran for President I did not originally embrace the idea. Looking back I think I was unwilling to see him in the light of a

President although his many achievements made clear he was a strong leader. Over time I realized that we have been trained to see only what politicians want us to see. That is dangerous to our freedom.

For years we had witnessed the decline of American manufacturing jobs and an apology tour that should have embarrassed Americans. Our educational system was corrupted by ideals that represented people who hate our country. Clear warnings were sounded but most ignored them. I hope it isn't too late to replace the pride in America that past generations all felt. Loving our country is essential to its survival.

In 2015 I watched antics that were embarrassing from our media and recognized leaders. It was childlike bullying at best. My mother was a serous journalist, retiring from the Cincinnati Enquirer. Most of my life was filled with the reasons why a journalist must be fair and impartial. She warned all of us to never pay attention to any newscaster whose political opinion was obvious; that is the determining factor in biases. She lined wastepaper baskets with corrupt newspapers. By the time Donald Trump broke into the political scene it was difficult to find any who met this criteria.

I have to question why, after almost four years of incredible successes by the President, is there such an effort to destroy him, still. Why is this necessary and who gains from it? The rhetoric from the media and the Democrat Party now includes Socialism. The idea of Communism is not nearly as shocking as it was in 2015. This should give great pause to any American who loves their country. The more times those words are used, the less shock effect it has.

I eventually embraced Donald Trump by his deeds with not so much attention to his style. I have since come to enjoy his bombastic, brutal honesty as we learned most of everything he suggested that has seemed outrageous was true. The facts we learned made it far easier to understand why so many people believed he must be destroyed. Those who engaged in that practice were soon exposed as the ones with the most to lose when the truth was exposed.

My hope is that the reader will set aside political affiliations and examine facts. I'm banking on the American DNA; that we will all be willing to stand tall and defend that which we know is right. I hope we will no longer be willing to be duped and corralled like cows, told what to believe, which will surely be followed by, 'sit down and shut up.' That is not the way of the American Patriots who came before us. We are honor bound to listen without bias. They have entrusted a treasure more valuable than the gold of Babylon to the US citizens.

This is the 32nd book I have written, another one is coming soon. I have more than 500 published articles available today. Please visit my website at arkconnect.com to learn more about the current books and articles.

Alexa Keating

Alexa Keating

Made in the USA
Coppell, TX
06 April 2023